THIRD EDITION

WORLDLINK

Developing English Fluency

Intro

James R. Morgan

Nancy Douglas

NATIONAL
GEOGRAPHIC
LEARNING | CENGAGE
Learning·

Australia • Brazil • Mexico • Singapore • United Kingdom • United States

**World Link Intro: Developing English Fluency,
Third Edition**
Nancy Douglas, Author
James R. Morgan, Author
Susan Stempleski, Series Editor

Publisher: Sherrise Roehr

Managing Editor: Sarah Kenney

Senior Development Editor: Margarita Matte

Development Editor: Brenden Layte

Associate Development Editor: Alison Bruno

Assistant Editor: Patricia Giunta

Media Researcher: Leila Hishmeh

Director, Digital Content: Aron Keesbury

Senior Technology Product Manager:
  Lauren Krolick

Director of Global Marketing: Ian Martin

Senior Product Marketing Manager:
  Caitlin Thomas

Sr. Director, ELT & World Languages:
  Michael Burggren

Production Manager: Daisy Sosa

Content Project Managers: Andrea Bobotas,
  Jen Coppens, Beth Houston

Senior Print Buyer: Mary Beth Hennebury

Composition: Lumina

Cover/Text Design: Brenda Carmichael

Art Director: Brenda Carmichael

Creative Director: Chris Roy

Cover Image: Eduardo Kobra

Inside Front Cover Image: AFP/Getty Images

Photo Credits are listed on the inside back cover.

For product information and technology assistance, contact us at
Cengage Learning Customer & Sales Support, 1-800-354-9706
For permission to use material from this text or product,
submit all requests online at **www.cengage.com/permissions**
Further permissions questions can be emailed to
permissionrequest@cengage.com

World Link Intro ISBN: 978-1-305-64774-9

World Link Intro + My World Link Online ISBN: 978-1-305-64775-6

National Geographic Learning
20 Channel Center Street
Boston, MA 02210
USA

Cengage Learning is a leading provider of customized learning solutions with employees residing in nearly 40 different countries and sales in more than 125 countries around the world. Find your local representative at **www.cengage.com**

Cengage Learning products are represented in Canada by Nelson Education, Ltd.

Visit National Geographic Learning online at ngl.cengage.com
Visit our corporate website at **cengage.com**

Printed in the United States of America
Print Number: 04   Print Year: 2018

Acknowledgments

We would like to extend a very special thank you to the Instituto Cultural Peruano Norteamericano (ICPNA) academic management staff in the central office, branches and teachers, for the helpful insights and suggestions that contributed toward the development of this series.

We would also like to thank Raúl Billini, Educational Consultant, Santo Domingo, Dominican Republic, for his contributions to this series.

Thank you to the educators who provided invaluable feedback throughout the development of the *World Link* series: Rocio Abarca, Instituto Tecnológico de Costa Rica / FUNDATEC; David Aduviri, CBA (Centro Boliviano Americano) - La Paz; Ramon Aguilar, Universidad Tecnológica de Hermosillo; Miguel Arrazola, CBA (Centro Boliviano Americano) - Santa Cruz; Cecilia Avila, Universidad de Xalapa; Isabel Baracat, CCI (Centro de Comunicação Inglesa); Daniel Sanchez Bedoy, Calfornia Language Center; Andrea Brotto, CEICOM (Centro de Idiomas para Comunidades); George Bozanich, Soongsil University; Emma Campo, Universidad Central; Andrea Carlson, Aichi Prefectural University; Martha Carrasco, Universidad Autonoma de Sinaloa; Herbert Chavel, Korea Advanced Institute of Science and Technology; J. Ventura Chavez, Universidad de Guadalajara CUSUR; Denise de Bartolomeo, AMICANA (Asociación Mendocina de Intercambio Cultural Argentino Norteamericano); Rodrigo de Campos Rezende, SEVEN Idiomas; John Dennis, Hokuriku University; Kirvin Andrew Dyer, Yan Ping High School; Marilena Fernandes, Alumni; Mark Firth, J.F. Oberlin University; Daniela Frillochi, ARICANA (Asociación Rosarina de Intercambio Cultural Argentino Norteamericano); Joseph Gabriella, Toyo University; Marina Gonzalez, Instituto Universitario de Lenguas Modernas; Robert Gordon, Korea Advanced Institute of Science and Technology; Scott Grigas, Youngsan University; Gu Yingruo, Research Institute of Xiangzhou District, ZhuHai; Kyle Hammel, Incheon National University; Mariana Gil Hammer, Instituto Cultural Dominico Americano; Helen Hanae, Toyo University; Xu Heng, Nantong Polytechnic College; Amiris Helena, Centro Cultural Dominico Americano; Rafael Hernandez, Centro Educacional Tlaquepaque; Yo-Tien Ho, Takming University; Marie Igwe, Hanseo University; Roxana Jimenez, Instituto Tecnológico de Costa Rica / FUNDATEC; Liu Jing, Shanghai Foreign Language Education Press; Lâm Nguyễn Huỳnh, Van Lang University; Hui-Chuan Liao, National Kaohsiung University of Applied Sciences; Pan Lang, Nanjing Sport Institute; Sirina Kainongsuang, Perfect Publishing Company Limited; Karen Ko, ChinYi University; Ching-Hua Lin, National Taiwan University of Science and Technology; Simon Liu, ChinYi University; Maria Helena Luna, Tronwell; Ady Marrero, Alianza Cultural Uruguay Estados Unidos; Nancy Mcaleer, ELC Universidad Interamericana de Panama; Michael McCallister, Feng Chia University Language Center; José Antonio Mendes Lopes, ICBEU (Instituto Cultural Brasil Estados Unidos); Tania Molina, Instituto Tecnológico de Costa Rica / FUNDATEC; Iliana Mora, Instituto Tecnológico de Costa Rica / FUNDATEC; Fernando Morales, Universidad Tecnológica de Hermosillo; Vivian Morghen, ICANA (Instituto Cultural Argentino Norteamericano); Aree Na Nan, Chiang Mai University; He Ning, Nanjing Mochou Vocational School; Paul Nugent, Kkottongnae University; Niu Yuchun, New Oriental School Beijing; Elizabeth Ortiz, COPEI (Copol English Institute); Virginia Ortiz, Universidad Autonoma de Tamaulipas; Marshall Presnick, Language Link Vietnam; Justin Prock, Pyeongtaek University; Peter Reilly, Universidad Bonaterra; Ren Huijun, New Oriental School Hangzhou; Andreina Romero, URBE (Universidad Rafael Belloso Chacín); Leon Rose, Jeonju University; Chris Ruddenklau, Kinki University; Adelina Ruiz, Instituto Tecnologico de Estudios Superiores de Occidente; Eleonora Salas, IICANA (Instituto de Intercambio Cultural Argentino Norteamericano); Jose Salas, Universidad Tecnológica del Norte de Guanajuato; Mary Sarawit, Naresuan University International College; Jenay Seymour, Hong-ik University; Huang Shuang, Shanghai International Studies University; Sávio Siqueira, ACBEU (Asociação Cultural Brasil Estados Unidos) / UFBA (Universidade Federal da Bahia); Beatriz Solina, ARICANA (Asociación Rosarina de Intercambio Cultural Argentino Norteamericano); Mari Cruz Suárez, Servicio de Idiomas UAM; Bambang Sujianto, Intensive English Course (IEC); Howard Tarnoff, Health Sciences University of Hokkaido; Emily J. Thomas, Incheon National University; Sandrine Ting, St. John's University; Tran Nguyen Hoai Chi, Vietnam USA Society English Training Service Center; Ruth Tun, Universidad Autonoma de Campeche; Rubén Uceta, Centro Cultural Dominico Americano; Maria Inés Valsecchi, Universidad Nacional de Río Cuarto; Alicia Vazquez, Instituto Internacional; Patricia Veciño, ICANA (Instituto Cultural Argentino Norteamericano); Punchalee Wasanasomsithi, Chulalongkorn University; Tomoe Watanabe, Hiroshima City University; Dhunyawat Treenate, Rajamangala University of Technology Krungthep; Haibo Wei, Nantong Agricultural College; Tomohiro Yanagi, Chubu University; Jia Yuan, Global IELTS School; Selestin Zainuddin, LBPP-LIA.

SCOPE & SEQUENCE

Grammar	Pronunciation	Speaking	Reading	Writing	Communication
* Subject pronouns and possessive adjectives with *be* pp. 8, 195 * *Yes / No* questions and short answers with *be* pp. 14, 196	Contractions with *be* p. 7	Introducing yourself p. 7	Famous name changers p. 12 Read for details Scan for information	Write about favorites p. 15	* Complete forms with personal information; Interview classmates p. 9 * Ask and answer questions about favorites p. 15
* Questions and answers with *who* and *where* pp. 22, 197 * Adjectives with *be* pp. 28, 198	Stressed syllables p. 19	Asking where someone is from p. 21	A great place to visit p. 26 Scan for information Read for details	Describe a favorite place p. 28	* Ask and answer questions about places p. 23 * Choose a vacation spot p. 29
* Spelling rules for forming plural nouns pp. 36, 199 * *This / that / these / those* pp. 42, 200	Plural endings p. 36	Giving and replying to thanks p. 35	The one thing I can't live without p. 40 Infer information Scan for information	Read and describe a product review p. 43	* Give and receive gifts p. 37 * Rate a product p. 43 Collect data in a chart
* The present continuous tense: affirmative and negative statements pp. 54, 201 * The present continuous tense: extended time pp. 60, 202	Question intonation p. 52	Greeting people and asking how they are p. 53	Study abroad p. 58 Identify main ideas Infer meaning Find key details	Answer interview questions p. 61	* Play charades p. 55 Act out and identify actions * A student interview p. 61 Interview classmates
* Simple present tense: affirmative and negative statements pp. 68, 203 * Simple present *Yes / No* questions and answers pp. 74, 204	*And, or* p. 66	Talking about likes and dislikes p. 67	Two powerful health foods p. 72 Scan for information Read for details	Write about a favorite food p. 75	* Plan a dinner party p. 69 Create a seating chart for guests according to personal information * Talk about your favorite food p. 75 Express agreement and disagreement
* Possessive nouns pp. 82, 205 * *Have got* pp. 88, 206	Possessive nouns: *'s* p. 82	Asking and answering questions about family p. 81	Time to get married? p. 86 Make predictions Read for details	Write about your family p. 89	* Famous families p. 83 Research and talk about family members * Take a relationship survey p. 89 Take a survey and explain answers Discuss results

SCOPE & SEQUENCE

Grammar	Pronunciation	Speaking	Reading	Writing	Communication
* Prepositions of time: *in, on, at, from... to* pp. 100, 207 * Simple present *Wh-* questions pp. 106, 207	Numbers: stress; *-ty* and *-teen* p. 98	Making suggestions p. 99	What kind of weekend person are you? p. 104 Make predictions Check predictions Read for specific information	Make plans p. 107	* Make a schedule and find time to meet with classmates p. 101 * Interview classmates about weekend activities p. 107
* Prepositions of time: *in* and *on* pp. 114, 208 * *When* and *How long* questions pp. 120, 209	Ordinal numbers: *th* and *t* p. 112	Saying you know or don't know something p. 113	Burning Man p. 118 Infer information Scan for information Read for details	Write about a festival p. 121	* Talk about holidays and special occasions p. 115 * Give a class presentation about a festival p. 121
* Frequency adverbs pp. 128, 210 * Review: simple present *Wh-* questions pp. 134, 211	Sentence stress p. 126	Apologizing p. 127	Dating Q & A with students around the world p. 132 Understand the main idea Read for details Read for opinions	Write about a good place for a date p. 135	* Role-play interviewing a roommate p. 129 * Give opinions about different types of dates p. 135
* *There is / There are* pp. 146, 212 * *Very / too* pp. 152, 213	Rising intonation to show surprise p. 144	Showing surprise p. 145	The power of color p. 150 Make predictions Check predictions Scan for information	Describe where you live p. 153	* Describe the location of objects in a room p. 147 * Identify and fix problems with a room p. 153
* *Want to / have to* pp. 160, 214 * Count and noncount nouns pp. 166, 215	*Want to* and *have to* p. 160	Saying what you want; asking for and giving prices p. 159	What do I pack? p. 164 Make predictions Read for details Infer meaning	Describe clothing p. 167	* Ask and answer questions about clothing p. 161 * Talk about and create fashion inventions p. 167
* Questions with *like* pp. 174, 216 * Talking about ability with *can / can't* pp. 180, 217	Reduced words p. 173	Talking about jobs p. 173	Internet entrepreneur Michelle Phan p. 178 Make predictions Read for details Scan for information	Write about personal work goals p. 181	* Exchange business cards and personal information p. 175 * Interview a partner about his or her job skills p. 181

Language Summaries p. 186   Grammar Notes p. 195

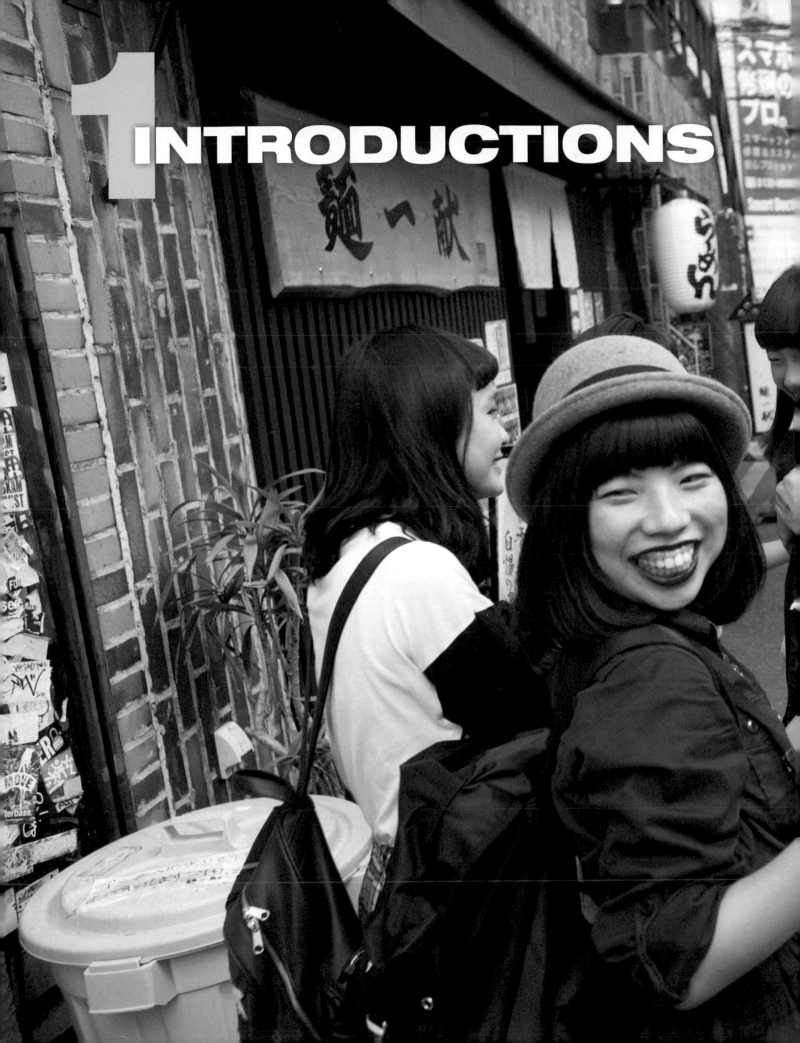

1 INTRODUCTIONS

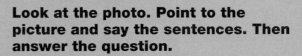

Look at the photo. Point to the picture and say the sentences. Then answer the question.

1 They are students.

2 They are friends.

3 Her name is Aya.

4 What's your name?

UNIT GOALS

1 Introduce yourself

2 Describe and answer questions about yourself and other people

3 Talk about your favorite TV shows, sports, and music

4 Read and spell email addresses

A group of students in Osaka, Japan

Students say "Hi" outside of school.

1 **VIDEO** Carlos's Day

A ▶ Watch the video. Repeat the sentences aloud as you watch.

B ▶ Watch the video again. This time, some sentences will be blank. Match the correct answers to complete the conversation.

1. _____   a. She's a student.
2. _____   b. See you!
3. _____   c. Hi!
4. _____   d. Bye!
5. _____   e. Hello!
6. _____   f. He's a student.

C Now say "Hi" and "Bye" to a partner.

2 VOCABULARY

A Complete the ID cards. Use the class list below.

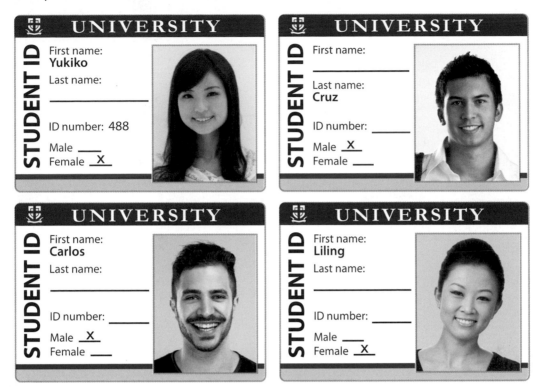

Class List: English 101		
Last name	**First name**	**Student ID number**
Akita	Yukiko	488
Cruz	Alberto	307
Ramalho	Carlos	592
Wong	Liling	169

Numbers 0–10

0 zero	4 four	8 eight
1 one	5 five	9 nine
2 two	6 six	10 ten
3 three	7 seven	

B 🔊 Listen. Check your answers. **CD 1 Track 2**

C 🔄 Make a student ID card for a partner. Ask him or her these questions.

What's your first name?

What's your last name?

What's your ID number?

3 LISTENING

A 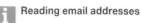 Answer the questions with a partner.

1. How do you spell your name?

2. Do you have a nickname (another name) or a short name?

3. What is your email address?

> My last name is Diaz.

> How do you spell that?

> It's spelled D-I-A-Z.

i Reading email addresses

@ = "at"
.com = "dot com"
.edu = "dot e-d-u"

Common types of email addresses

(business name) .com
(school name) .edu
(organization name) .org

B 🔊 **Listen for details**. Listen. Fill in the nicknames. Then fill in Joshua's last name.
CD 1 Track 3

HELLO

1. My name is ____Joshua____.

In this class, call me: _____.

HELLO

2. My name is ____Yukiko Akita____.

In this class, call me: _____.

Email address: Yukiko@_____

HELLO

3. My name is ____Alberto Cruz____.

In this class, call me: _____.

Email address: Alberto@_____

HELLO

4. My name is ____Liling Wong____.

In this class, call me: _____.

Email address: Liling@_____

C 🔊 Listen to the full conversation. Complete the email addresses. **CD 1 Track 4**

D 🔄 Say and spell the names and email addresses of each person with a partner.

4 SPEAKING

A 🔊 🔁 **Pronunciation: Contractions with _be_.** Practice saying these full and contracted (shorter) forms with a partner. Then listen and repeat. **CD 1 Track 5**

I am → I'm → I'm a student.

What is → What's → What's your name?

It is → It's → It's nice to meet you.

B 🔊 **Pronunciation: Contractions with _be_.** Say the words in blue with your instructor. Then listen to the audio. Circle the words you hear. **CD 1 Track 6**

1. A: Hi, I am / I'm Ken.

   B: What is / What's your last name, Ken?

   A: It is / It's Tanaka.

   B: Great. And what is / what's your student ID number?

   A: It's 524.

2. A: What is / What's your name, please?

   B: It is / It's Maria Fuentes.

   A: Hmmm, you are / you're not on my class list. Your last name is Fuentes?

   B: Yes, that is / that's right.

C 🔁 **Pronunciation: Contractions with _be_.** Practice the dialogs in **B** with a partner.

D 🔊 🔁 Listen to the conversation. Then practice with a partner. **CD 1 Track 7**

LILING: Hi, my name's Liling. What's your name?

ALBERTO: Hi, Liling. I'm Alberto, but please call me Beto. It's my nickname.

LILING: Okay, Beto. Nice to meet you.

ALBERTO: It's nice to meet you, too.

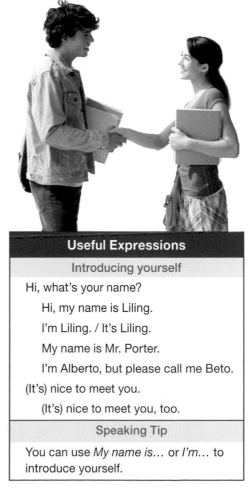

E 🔁 Practice the conversation again with your partner. Use your own names.

SPEAKING STRATEGY

F 👥 Use the Useful Expressions. Meet six classmates. Write their names in the box.

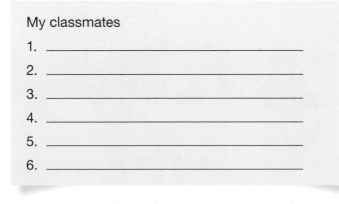

My classmates

1. _____
2. _____
3. _____
4. _____
5. _____
6. _____

Useful Expressions
Introducing yourself
Hi, what's your name?
Hi, my name is Liling.
I'm Liling. / It's Liling.
My name is Mr. Porter.
I'm Alberto, but please call me Beto.
(It's) nice to meet you.
(It's) nice to meet you, too.
Speaking Tip
You can use _My name is…_ or _I'm…_ to introduce yourself.

G 🔁 Say your classmates' names to a partner.

5 GRAMMAR

A   Turn to page 195. Complete the exercises. Then do **B** and **C** below.

Subject Pronouns with *be*			
Subject pronoun	***be***		**Subject pronoun contractions with *be***
I	**am**		I am = I'm
You	**are**	a student.	you are = you're
He / She	**is**		he is = he's / she is = she's

Possessive Adjectives with *be*			
Possessive adjective		***be***	
My			
Your	last name	**is**	Smith.
His / Her			

B   Look at the pictures. Then play the memory game with your class. How far can you go?

1 My name is Rina. I'm a student.

2 Your name is Rina. You are a student. My name is Lucas. I am a student.

3 Your name is Rina. You are a student. Your name is Lucas. You are a student. My name is Jen. I am a student.

C   Play again. This time use numbers and *he, his*, *she,* and *her*.

1 My name is Rina. I am a student. My number is 8.

2 Her name is Rina. She is a student. Her number is 8. My name is Lucas. I am a student. My number is 3.

3 Her name is Rina. She is a student. Her number is 8. His name is Lucas. He is a student. His number is 3. My name is Jen....

6 COMMUNICATION

A Look at the answers. Write the correct questions.

1. What's _____?

   My name is Ariana Valdez.

2. _____?

   My email address is avaldez@eazypost.com.

3. _____?

   My phone number is (399) 555-7061.

B Imagine you are a new student. Make up a new name, phone number, and email address. Complete the form.

The English School of Melbourne, Australia

Last name _____   First name _____

(613) _____
Phone number   Email address

C Meet four students. Write their information below. Use your "new" information from above.

Student 1
Last name: _____
First name: _____
Phone number: _____
Email address: _____

Student 3
Last name: _____
First name: _____
Phone number: _____
Email address: _____

Student 2
Last name: _____
First name: _____
Phone number: _____
Email address: _____

Student 4
Last name: _____
First name: _____
Phone number: _____
Email address: _____

Chrissy Martinez

Chrissy | Home

Friends • 300

Music • 2

Pitbull   Adele

Sports • 2

FC Barcelona   Lionel Messi

Movies • 1

The Hunger Games

TV Shows • 1

Sherlock

1 VOCABULARY

A Look at the boxes. Then think of two other kinds of music and sports. Tell a partner.

B Look at Chrissy's web page above. Complete the sentences with a partner.

1. Chrissy **is friends with** _____ people.
2. Her **favorite sport** is _____.
3. Her favorite **player** is _____.
4. Her favorite kinds of **music** are _____ and _____.
5. Her favorite **TV show** is _____.
6. Her favorite **singers** are _____ and _____.
7. Her favorite **movie** is _____.
8. Her favorite **actor** is Benedict Cumberbatch. Her favorite _____ is Jennifer Lawrence.

C Talk about your friends and favorite things. Make eight sentences like the ones in **B**. Tell a partner.

Music
classical
pop
rap
rock

Sports
baseball
basketball
soccer
tennis

My favorite TV show is....

2 LISTENING

A 🔄 Point to a photo. Use one of the sentences below to describe it to a partner. Take turns.

> It's a reality show.   It's a scary show.   It's a soccer game.

B 🔊 **Listen for gist.** Listen to a man and woman talk about shows on TV. Number each show (1, 2, or 3) as they talk about it. **CD 1 Track 8**

C 🔊 **Listen for details.** Listen again. Which show do they watch? Circle it. **CD 1 Track 8**

D 🔄 Do people watch shows like this in your country? What other shows are popular in your country? Tell a partner.

> Soccer is popular.

> ... is also popular.

3 READING

A 🔁 Look at the people. Do you know their names? Tell a partner.

B 🔁 **Read for details.** Work with a partner.

- **Student A:** Read about people 1 and 2.
  Student B: Read about people 3 and 4.
- Underline each person's nickname or new name.
  Circle his or her real or full name. For person 1, circle why nobody knows his real name.

C 🔁 **Scan for information.** Talk about one of your two people. Say the person's real or full name, and his or her nickname or new name. Your partner takes notes and asks questions.

> This is Paul Van Haver. He's a singer.

> What's his nickname?

> It's....

> Can you spell that, please?

D 🔁 Read about your partner's person or people. Check your answers in **C**.

WORLD LINK

Go online. Find one more famous name changer. What is his or her real or full name?

FAMOUS
NAME
CHANGERS

1 BANKSY is a street artist and filmmaker from the United Kingdom. No one knows his real name, and there are no pictures of him. This way he can do his work freely.

2 **GIVANILDO VIEIRA DE SOUSA** is a soccer player from Brazil. His nickname is Hulk. Why? He's very strong, but he also looks like The Hulk!

3 **J. K. ROWLING** is a writer and the author of the *Harry Potter* books. Her full name is Joanne Kathleen Rowling, but her friends call her Jo.

4 **PAUL VAN HAVER** is a famous hip-hop singer from Belgium, but everyone knows him as Stromae. The name *Stromae* comes from changing the sounds in the word *maestro*[1] from *mae – stro* to *stro – mae*.

[1]A *maestro* is a great musician.

4 GRAMMAR

A Turn to page 196. Complete the exercises. Then do **B** and **C** below.

Yes / No Questions with *be*			Short Answers	
be	Subject pronoun		Affirmative	Negative
Am	I	in this class?	Yes, you **are**.	No, you**'re not**. / No, you **aren't**.
Are	you	a student?	Yes, I **am**.	No, I**'m not**.
Is	he / she		Yes, he **is**.	No, he**'s not**. / No, he **isn't**.
Is	it	her real name?	Yes, it **is**.	No, it**'s not**. / No, it **isn't**.

B 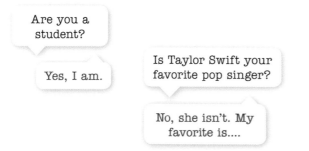 Complete the dialogs. Then practice them with a partner.

1. A: _____*Are you*_____ a student?

   B: Yes, _____.

2. A: _____ English your native language?

   B: No, _____.

3. A: _____ from this city?

   B: No, _____. I'm from Shanghai.

4. A: _____ Chris Hemsworth your favorite actor?

   B: No, _____.

5. A: _____ Taylor Swift your favorite pop singer?

   B: Yes, _____. Her music is great!

6. A: _____ friends with anyone from the US?

   B: Yes, _____. I have a friend who is from New York.

C 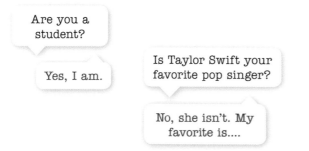 Ask a partner the six questions in **B**. This time, talk about yourselves.

Are you a student?

Yes, I am.

Is Taylor Swift your favorite pop singer?

No, she isn't. My favorite is....

5 WRITING

A Write six sentences. Write about your favorite...

actor / actress	sports player	movie
singer	TV show	website

B Write one of your sentences from above on a piece of paper. Give it to your instructor.

My favorite soccer player is Cristiano Ronaldo.

My favorite singer is Rihanna.

6 COMMUNICATION

A Your instructor will give you a classmate's sentence. Ask your classmates *Yes / No* questions. Find the writer of the sentence.

Is Cristiano Ronaldo your favorite soccer player?

No, he's not.

Yes, he is! It's my sentence.

B Repeat **A** with a different sentence.

2 COUNTRIES

Look at the photo. Answer the questions.

1 Name the place in the photo. Where is it?

2 Budapest is the capital of Hungary. What is the capital city of your country?

3 There are many tourists in Budapest. Are there many tourists in your city?

UNIT GOALS

1 Name cities and countries

2 Ask questions about people and places

3 Identify adjectives and nouns

4 Describe a city

The Parliament Building, Budapest, Hungary

A beach in Southern Thailand

1 **VIDEO** Speeding Around the World in Under Five Minutes

A 🔊 Listen. Say each country after the speaker. **CD 1 Track 10**

☐ Egypt ☐ Mexico ☐ Portugal ☐ Spain ☐ the United Kingdom
☐ Japan ☐ Peru ☐ South Korea ☐ Turkey ☐ the United States

B ▶ Watch the video. Check (✓) the countries in **A** that you see in the video. Two are extra.

C ▶ 🔄 Watch again. Say two other countries in the video. Do you remember any cities? Tell a partner.

D 🔄 Which place in the video is your favorite? Tell a partner.

2 VOCABULARY

Yusef

Mei Li

Sofia

Ji Ming

Diego

Ryan

A 🔊 **Pronunciation: Stressed syllables.** Listen and repeat. Say the countries and nationalities in the chart. **CD 1 Track 11**

B 🔊 **Pronunciation: Stressed syllables.** Listen and repeat again. Which nationalities have a different syllable stressed than the countries? Circle them in the chart. **CD 1 Track 11**

Country	Nationality
China	(Chinese)
Japan	Japanese
Portugal	Portuguese
Australia	Australian
Brazil	Brazilian
Peru	Peruvian
Korea	Korean
Mexico	Mexican
the United States	American
Spain	Spanish
the United Kingdom	British
Turkey	Turkish

The same syllable is stressed	A different syllable is stressed
Bra ZIL Bra ZIL ian	CHI na Chi NESE

C 🔄 Where is each World Cup fan from? What languages do they speak? Tell a partner. Use the words in the chart.

> Yusef is from Turkey.

> Yusef is Turkish. He speaks Turkish.

D 🔄 Where are you from? What language(s) do you speak? Tell a partner.

3 LISTENING

Machu Picchu

A 🔊 **Make predictions.** *Where in the World?* is a TV game show. Listen to each clue. Then circle the correct answer. **CD 1 Track 12**

1. a. the United States
   b. Canada
   c. Mexico

2. a. Canada
   b. Brazil
   c. the United Kingdom

3. a. Australia
   b. Argentina
   c. New Zealand

4. a. France
   b. the United States
   c. China

5. a. Brazil
   b. Chile
   c. Peru

6. a. Thailand
   b. Vietnam
   c. Malaysia

B 🔊 **Check predictions; Listen for details.** Listen. Check your answers in **A**. **CD 1 Track 13**

| ✓ | That's right. / That's correct. |
| ✗ | That's wrong. / That's incorrect. |

C ⚡ People from New Zealand are New Zealanders. They are also called "Kiwis." Look at your answers in **A**. Name each nationality.

4 SPEAKING

A  Listen to the conversation. Where is Ana from? Where is Haru from? **CD 1 Track 14**

HARU: Excuse me? Are you in this class?

ANA: Yes, I am. Are you?

HARU: Yeah. Hi, my name's <u>Haru</u>.

ANA: Hi, I'm <u>Ana</u>.

HARU: Great to meet you.

ANA: You, too. So, where are you from, <u>Haru</u>?

HARU: <u>Japan</u>.

ANA: Cool. Which city?

HARU: <u>Tokyo</u>. How about you? Where are you from?

ANA: <u>Bogotá, Colombia</u>.

Tokyo, Japan

B Now practice the conversation in **A** with a partner. Replace the underlined words with your own information.

SPEAKING STRATEGY

C Think of a famous person. Write his or her information below.

Name: _____

City and country: _____

D Imagine you are a famous person at a party. Meet three people using the Useful Expressions.

> Hi, I'm Rafael Nadal.

> Hi, Rafa. Where are you from?

> I'm from Spain.

> Really? Which city?

Useful Expressions
Asking where someone is from
Where are you from?
(I'm from) Japan.
Really? Where exactly? Which city?
(I'm from) Tokyo / a small town near Tokyo.
Are you from Colombia?
Yes, I am.
No, I'm from Peru.
Speaking Tip
Where in Japan?
Osaka.

A teahouse in Shanghai, China

5 GRAMMAR

A Turn to page 197. Complete the exercises. Then do **B–E** below.

Questions with *who*			Answers
Who	is / 's	with you?	Tomas (is).

Questions with *where*			Answers
Where	are	you / they?	(I'm / We're / They're) **at** the beach / a museum.
Where	is / 's	Nor?	(She's) **in** London. / **at** her hotel.
		Machu Picchu?	(It's) **in** Peru.

B   Nor is talking to Sara on the phone. Complete the dialog with *who, where, at,* or *in*. Then practice with a partner.

SARA: Hello?

NOR: <u>Sara</u>? Hi, it's <u>Nor</u>.

SARA: Hi, <u>Nor</u>! _____ are you?

NOR: I'm _____ <u>the UK</u>. Right now, I'm _____ <u>London</u>.

SARA: _____ exactly?

NOR: I'm _____ <u>Buckingham Palace</u>. Oh, and I'm here with a friend.

SARA: Really? _____'s with you?

NOR: <u>Irina</u>, from our English class. She lives _____ <u>London</u> now.

SARA: That's great! Say "Hi" for me.

C   Make two new conversations with a partner. Replace the underlined parts in **B** with the ideas below.

1. Use your names at the start and one of these two places.
   • Shanghai, China / a teahouse   • Punta Cana, the Dominican Republic / a beach

2. At the end, use a classmate's name.

D   Repeat Exercise **C**. Use a new city and place. Sit back-to-back with your partner and have the conversation. Try not to read the dialog.

E   Work with a new partner. Talk about your "phone call" in Exercise **D**. Where is your partner? Who is your partner with?

> Marta is in New York City with Diego. They're at the Statue of Liberty.

6 COMMUNICATION

A **Directions:** Play in pairs.

1. Put a marker (a coin, an eraser) on *Start Here*.

2. Take turns. Flip a coin.

   Heads: Move one square.
   Tails: Move two squares.

3. Answer the question. For *Free Question!,* your partner asks you about a city or country.

   Each correct answer = 1 point

4. Finish at square 24. The winner is the person with the most points.

Answers are on page 218.

Carnival

FUN FACTS ABOUT RIO DE JANEIRO, BRAZIL

Rio is a **large**, **old** city of 6.5 million people.

Its nickname is "the Marvelous City" because its beaches are **beautiful**, its nightlife is **exciting**, and its people are **friendly**.

Rio is **famous** for…

- Carnival: Every year the streets are **crowded** and **busy** with people from all over Brazil and the world.
- Copacabana: This is a **relaxing** beach. It's also a **popular** place to play soccer.
- Pão de Açúcar: This is a **big** mountain. It is 396 meters (1,300 feet) **tall**. From here, there's a **wonderful** view of the city.

Rio is an **interesting** city and a **fun** place to visit!

1 VOCABULARY

A 🔁 Look at the pictures and read about the city of Rio. Is your city the same or different? Tell a partner. Use the vocabulary words.

> My city isn't large, but it is old.

B 🔁 Answer the questions with a partner.

1. Is your city big or small?
2. Is it interesting?
3. Are the people friendly?
4. Are the streets crowded? If yes, where and when?
5. What is your city famous for?
6. What is your favorite place in your city? Why?

Copacabana and Pão de Açúcar

Word Bank
Opposites
big, large ↔ **small**
old ↔ **new**
interesting ↔ **boring**

2 LISTENING

Khaju Bridge, Isfahan

The Grand Bazaar, Isfahan

A 🔄 **Make predictions.** Answer the questions with a partner.

1. Look at the map. Say the countries together. What part of the world is this?

2. Look at the photos. What words describe these places? Use the words from page 24.

B 🔊 Listen to John talk about the city of Isfahan. Where is it? Write your answer: _____.
CD 1 Track 15

C 🔊 **Listen for details.** Listen. Match the places (1–5) to the words that describe them (a–h). Some will have more than one answer. **CD 1 Track 16**

1. Iran _____
2. Iranians _____
3. Khaju Bridge _____
4. the main square _____
5. Isfahan _____

    a. beautiful   e. wonderful
    b. big   f. old
    c. famous   g. relaxing
    d. friendly   h. interesting

D 🔄 Do you want to visit Isfahan? Why or why not? Tell a partner.

3 READING

A 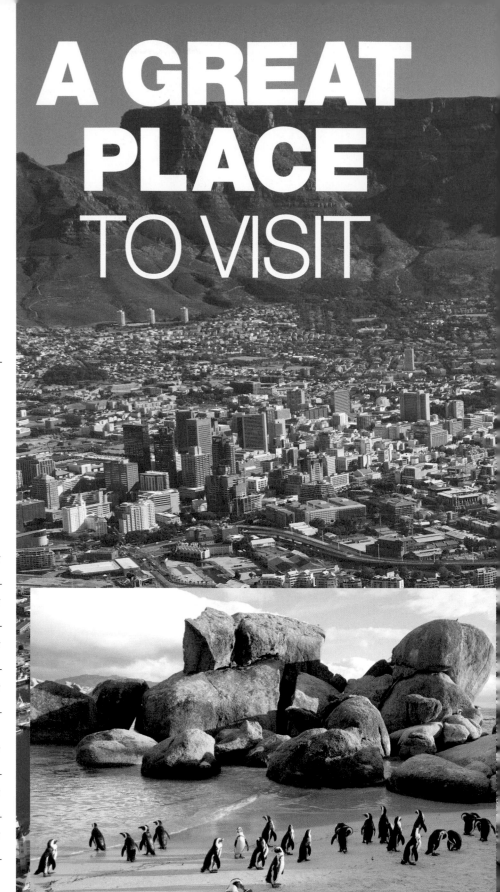 In one minute, write down any famous cities and places in your country on a piece of paper. Compare your lists with a partner's. Why are the places famous?

B **Scan for information.** Read the email. Where is Melissa? In which city and country? Follow the steps below to guess.

1. Circle key words.
2. Write your guess:
   _____
3. 🔄 Compare your answer with a partner's.
4. Check your answer at the bottom of the next page.

C **Read for details.** Read Melissa's note. Circle T for *True* or F for *False*. Correct the false sentences to make them true.

1. Melissa is in Sydney.   T   F
   _____
2. She's on vacation.   T   F
   _____
3. She's in a big city.   T   F
   _____
4. Long Street is not busy.   T   F
   _____
5. Penguins are on Table Mountain.   T   F
   _____
6. Melissa loves soccer.   T   F
   _____
7. Her vacation is fun.   T   F
   _____

WORLD LINK

Go online and find one more fact about this city. Tell your partner about it. Would you like to visit here? Why or why not?

A GREAT PLACE TO VISIT

Penguins at Boulders Beach

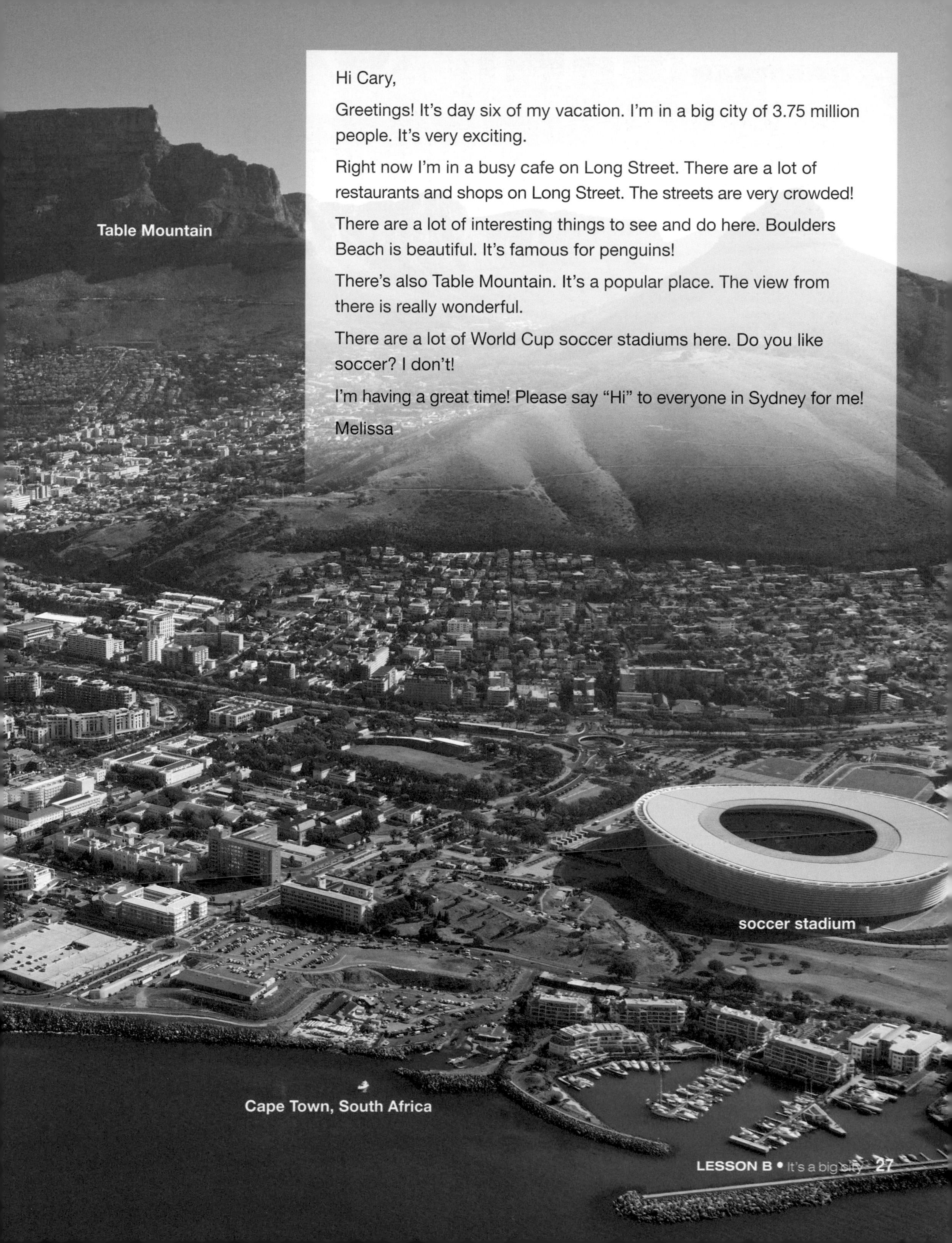

Hi Cary,

Greetings! It's day six of my vacation. I'm in a big city of 3.75 million people. It's very exciting.

Right now I'm in a busy cafe on Long Street. There are a lot of restaurants and shops on Long Street. The streets are very crowded!

There are a lot of interesting things to see and do here. Boulders Beach is beautiful. It's famous for penguins!

There's also Table Mountain. It's a popular place. The view from there is really wonderful.

There are a lot of World Cup soccer stadiums here. Do you like soccer? I don't!

I'm having a great time! Please say "Hi" to everyone in Sydney for me!

Melissa

Table Mountain

soccer stadium

Cape Town, South Africa

Adjectives with *be*							
	be	Adjective			*be*	Adjective	Noun
Your city	**is**	beautiful.	It		**is**	an exciting	city.
The buildings	**are**	old.	There		**are**	many tall	buildings.

A Turn to page 198. Complete the exercises. Then do **B–E** below.

B 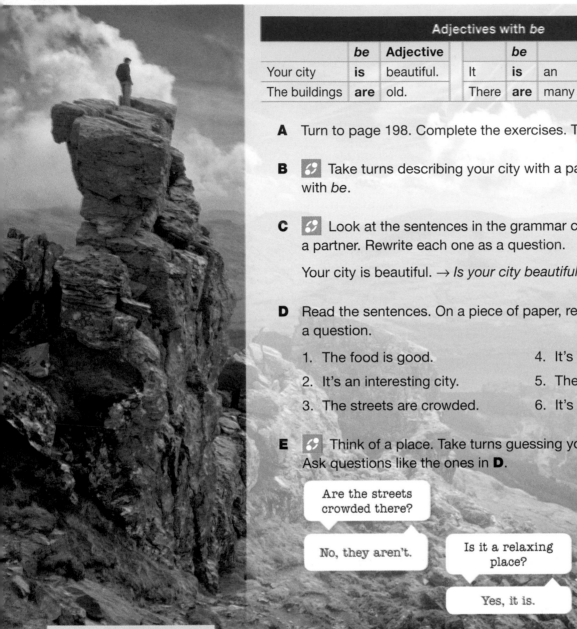 Take turns describing your city with a partner. Use adjectives with *be*.

C Look at the sentences in the grammar chart above. Work with a partner. Rewrite each one as a question.

Your city is beautiful. → *Is your city beautiful?*

D Read the sentences. On a piece of paper, rewrite each one as a question.

1. The food is good.
2. It's an interesting city.
3. The streets are crowded.
4. It's busy and exciting.
5. The people are friendly.
6. It's famous for music.

E Think of a place. Take turns guessing your partner's place. Ask questions like the ones in **D**.

> Are the streets crowded there?

> No, they aren't.

> Is it a relaxing place?

> Yes, it is.

A hiker in Arrochar, Scotland

5 WRITING

A You are going to write about your favorite place. First, answer these questions on a piece of paper.

1. What is the name of your favorite place?
2. Where is it?
3. What are two adjectives that describe it?
4. What is it famous for?

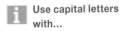 **Use capital letters with...**
- people and place names
- countries and languages

Bedugul, Bali

B Write about your favorite place. Use your notes in **A**.

My favorite place is Montreal. It's in Canada. People speak English and French there. It's famous for churches and ice hockey. Montreal is busy with people from around the world. The French food is good, too!

C Exchange papers with a partner. Check for capital letters. Do you want to visit your partner's place?

6 COMMUNICATION

A Look at the map and photo. Where is Bali—in which country? Is it a good place for a vacation?

B Where is a good place for a vacation? Write your ideas in the chart under *My idea*.

	My idea	My classmate's idea	My classmate's idea	My classmate's idea
Place				
Where is it?				
How is it there?				

C Interview three classmates. Complete the rest of the chart.

D Choose one place for a vacation. Explain your choice to a partner.

> It's a good place for a vacation. The beaches are beautiful, the people are friendly, and the nightlife is fun.

3 POSSESSIONS

A man sits in front of his car, Trinidad, Cuba.

Look at the photo. Answer the questions.

1 What is the man's favorite thing?

2 Is it old or new?

3 What is your favorite thing?

UNIT GOALS

1 Identify everyday objects

2 Give and reply to thanks

3 Talk about having more than one of something

4 Use adjectives to describe and rate items

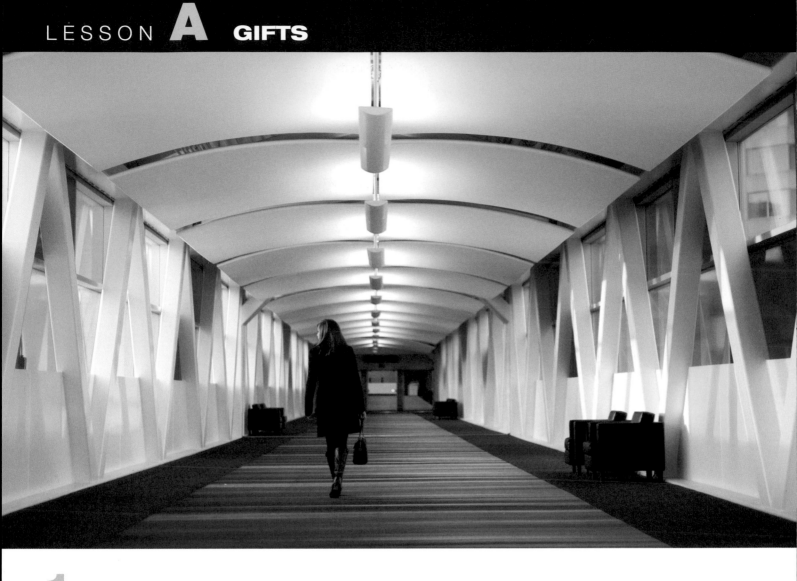

1 **VIDEO** What Do You Carry With You?

A  Look at the photo and the title of the video. Guess: What is the video about? Circle your answer. Tell a partner.

a. gifts   b. important items   c. friends

B ▶ Watch the video. Check your answer in **A**.

C ▶ What items are in the video? Check (✓) the ones you see.

☐ a photo   ☐ keys   ☐ a cell phone   ☐ a map
☐ candy   ☐ a computer   ☐ a ring   ☐ a wallet
☐ a book   ☐ a soccer ball ☐ an apple   ☐ a camera

D 🔄 What do you carry with you? Tell a partner.

I always carry a book.

2 VOCABULARY

A Match each item in the list with an item on the website. Write the numbers on the website.

1. a **backpack**
2. a **camera**
3. a **gift card**
4. **headphones**
5. a **wallet**
6. an **expensive watch**

gift link.com   🔍 Search for gifts   HOME   SALE   CUSTOMER SERVICE   🛒 CART

Gift ideas >> Graduation gifts for students >> Most popular

B  Look at the gifts. With a partner, ask and answer a question about each one.

> What's this?
>
> A watch.

C Answer these questions with a partner.

1. What items in **A** do you have?
2. What is the best gift for a student?
3. Which of these gifts is your favorite?

3 LISTENING

A 🔊 **Listen for details.** Listen and circle the correct answers. **CD 1 Track 18**

1. Sue is Tak's classmate / friend.
2. Tak is buying her a graduation / birthday gift.
3. Sue likes baseball / tennis / soccer.
4. She likes hip-hop / pop music.

Word Bank
birthday = day someone was born
brand = category of products made by a company

B 🔊 **Listen for sequence.** Listen. Number the items as you hear them. (You will not number all of the items.) **CD 1 Track 19**

a backpack _____   a camera _____

headphones _____   a watch _____

a wallet _____   a gift card _____

C 🔊 Listen. Does Tak buy each item? Why or why not? Check and circle your answers. **CD 1 Track 20**

1. ☐ buys ☐ doesn't buy   It's a boring / fun gift.

2. ☐ buys ☐ doesn't buy   It's a nice / an expensive gift.

3. ☐ buys ☐ doesn't buy   They're popular / her favorite brand.

WORLD LINK

What's a popular graduation gift in your country? Go online. Find some examples.

4 SPEAKING

A 🔊 👥 Listen to the conversation. Then practice it with two partners. **CD 1 Track 21**

SUN: Oh, no...

PAULA: What's wrong, Sun?

SUN: My wallet. Where's my <u>wallet</u>?

PAULA: Is it in your pocket?

SUN: Um... no.

PAULA: What about your backpack?

SUN: No, it's not. I can't find it anywhere!

MAN: Hmm... what's this? Excuse me, miss?

SUN: Yes?

MAN: Is this your <u>wallet</u>?

SUN: Yes, it is! Thank you very much!

MAN: You're welcome.

B 👥 Practice the conversation again. Take a different role. Replace the underlined word in **A** to ask about the items below.

key

student ID

bus pass

SPEAKING STRATEGY

C 🔄 Imagine you lost one of the important items below. Create a short dialog. Thank and reply to each other formally.

D 🔄 Repeat the dialog in **C**. This time, thank and reply to each other informally.

Useful Expressions		
Giving and replying to thanks		
Saying _Thank you_		**Replies**
Thank you very much.	**formal**	You're welcome.
Thank you.	↑	My pleasure.
Thanks a lot.	↓	Sure, no problem.
Thanks.	**informal**	You bet.

a credit card

a cell phone

a notebook

a laptop

 **GRAMMAR**

A Turn to page 199. Complete the exercises. Then do **B** and **C** below.

Spelling Rules for Forming Plural Nouns		
Most plural nouns are formed by adding *s*:	camera → camera**s**	pen → pen**s**
For nouns ending in a <u>vowel</u> + *y* add *s*:	bo**y** → bo**ys**	
but For nouns ending in a <u>consonant</u> + *y*, drop the *y* and add *ies*:	dictionar**y** → dictionar**ies**	
For nouns ending in a <u>vowel</u> + *o* add *s*:	rad**io** → rad**io**s	
but For nouns ending in a <u>consonant</u> + *o*, add *s* with some nouns and *es* with others:	pho**to** → pho**tos**	pota**to** → pota**toes**
For nouns ending in *ch, sh, ss,* or *x,* add *es:*	cla**ss** → cla**sses**	
For nouns ending in *f / fe,* change it to *ve* + *s*:	kni**fe** → kni**ves**	lea**f** → lea**ves**

B 🔊 **Pronunciation: Plural endings.** Listen and repeat. Then practice saying the singular and plural forms of the nouns. **CD 1 Track 22**

<u>Group 1</u>

class → classes   wish → wishes
watch → watches   language → languages

<u>Group 2</u>

backpack → backpacks   laptop → laptops
notebook → notebooks   wallet → wallets

<u>Group 3</u>

camera → cameras   gift card → gift cards
key → keys   pen → pens

C 🔁 Read the rules of the guessing game. Then play the game with a partner.

1. Write the number *1* on five pieces of paper.
2. Write the number *2* on five pieces of paper.
3. Mix up the pieces of paper and place them face down.
4. Choose a word from the list in Exercise **B** and pick up a piece of paper.
5. Draw one or two pictures of your word (for example *one pen* or *two backpacks*).
6. Your partner guesses the answer and then spells out the word.

> The answer is backpacks.
> B-A-C-K-P-A-C-K-S.

6 COMMUNICATION

A 🔁 Practice the conversation with a partner.

LUCAS: Oh, let's see.... What's this? Wow, it's a cool watch. Thanks, Jane. I really like it.

JANE: No problem, Lucas. I'm glad you like it.

B 🔁 Practice the conversation again with a different gift idea and way of saying *Thank you*.

When people say *Thank you* for a gift, they also say...		
Thanks.	I really like it / them.	
	I like it / them a lot.	
	It's They're	cool / beautiful / great / nice / perfect.

C Think of a gift. Write the name of the gift on a small piece of paper. Fold the paper.

a watch

sunglasses

D 🔁 Follow these gift-giving steps.

1. Exchange the gifts you wrote in **C** with a partner. Thank your partner. Write the name of the gift in the box below.

2. Exchange the gift you got with a new partner. Then do this three more times. Write each new gift in the box.

Gifts
1. _____
2. _____
3. _____
4. _____
5. _____

E 🔁 Tell a new partner about your gifts. Which is your favorite?

I got sunglasses, a watch, a laptop....

What's your favorite?

The laptop!

1 VOCABULARY

A 🔄 Look at the photo. Read the information. Then circle the correct word with a partner.

1. A pack rat's room is / isn't clean.

2. A pack rat keeps / throws out old things.

3. For a pack rat, only the expensive / cheap and expensive things are important.

B Complete the sentences. Make them true for you.

1. My room is / isn't messy.

2. It's hard / easy to find things in my room.

3. Usually, I keep / throw out old things.

4. True or False for you: Sometimes, I buy something because it's cheap, but I don't use it.

C 🔄 Tell a partner your answers in **B**. Are you similar to Laura?

> My room isn't messy. It's clean and comfortable.

Laura is a "pack rat." There are many old things in her room: clothes, bags, photos. She doesn't use these things anymore. Some of the things are expensive. But some things, like the clothes, are **cheap**. For Laura, they are all **important**. She **keeps** everything!

Laura's room is **messy**, and it's **hard** to find things. For you and me, her room is **uncomfortable**, but not for Laura! She likes it.

> The prefix **un** = **not**

Word Bank
Opposites
cheap ↔ expensive
comfortable ↔ uncomfortable
hard ↔ **easy**
important ↔ **unimportant**
keep ↔ **throw out**
messy ↔ **clean**

2 LISTENING

A **Make predictions.** Alison is cleaning her room. She is talking to her friend Mia about the things above. Guess: Which country are these things from? _____

B 🔊 **Listen for gist.** Listen. Number the things above (1, 2, 3) as you hear them. **CD 1 Track 23**

C 🔊 **Listen for details.** Listen again. Does Alison keep or throw out each thing? Why? Mark the correct answers. **CD 1 Track 23**

	Alison...		**Why?**
1.	☐ keeps it.	☐ throws it out.	It's clean / cool / old.
2.	☐ keeps it.	☐ throws it out.	It's a(n) nice / interesting / bad photo.
3.	☐ keeps it.	☐ throws it out.	It's from an expensive store.
			a good friend.
			a popular museum.

D ⚡ Do you keep any old things? Why? Tell a partner. Give an example.

3 READING

A 🔄 **Infer information.** Read the title, the sentences under it, and the boxed information. Guess: What is a photographer's most important item? What is an archaeologist's most important item?

B **Scan for information.** Read the article. Then follow the steps below.

 1. Circle each person's important item(s).

 2. Why is the item important to the person? Underline the answer.

C 🔄 With a partner, explain each person's most important item. Use your answers in **B**.

> Person 1 is Cory Richards. His most important item is....

D 🔄 What item is important to you? Why? Tell a partner. Are any answers the same in your class?

> It's my cell phone. There's a lot of important information on my phone.

Word Bank
📍 GPS
🎩 hat
🧴 sunscreen

WORLD LINK

Interview three people outside of class. What item is important to each person? Why? Tell the class. What answers are popular?

THE ONE THING I CAN'T LIVE WITHOUT

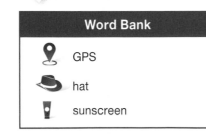

What item is very important to you? Five people from National Geographic share their ideas.

The people at *National Geographic*

A *photographer* takes pictures.

An *archaeologist* and a *paleoanthropologist* find and study very old humans and their cultures.

1 **CORY RICHARDS** is a photographer. A camera and a pencil are his most important items. They are common[1] items, but with these, he takes pictures and writes about his experiences.

2 **CARLTON WARD** is also a photographer. His camera is important to him, but his GPS is important, too. Ward works in different places around the world, and it's easy to get lost.[2] He uses the GPS to get directions.

3 Archaeologist **CHRIS THORNTON** works in places like South Africa and Oman. He is outside a lot. For this reason, his most important item is sunscreen. "It protects[3] my skin," he says.

4 **LEE BERGER** is a paleoanthropologist. He is also outside a lot. But his most important item isn't sunscreen; it's a comfortable hat. "It's my lucky hat," he says. When he wears it, he always finds something interesting.

5 Archaeologist **KUENGA WANGMO** also has a lucky item. It's a bracelet from Bhutan, her home country. It protects her, she says.

Carlton Ward

[1] If something is *common*, many people have it.
[2] If you are *lost*, you don't know where you are.
[3] If something *protects* you, it keeps you safe.

4 GRAMMAR

A Turn to page 200. Complete the exercises. Then do **B–D** below.

this / that / these / those	
What's **this** called in English?	It's a "cell phone."
Is **that** a new phone?	Yes, it is.
Are **these** your keys?	No, they're not.
Are **those** headphones comfortable?	Yes, they are.

B 🔁 Look in your backpack or bag. Put three or four things from it on your desk (for example, your keys, wallet, or phone). Then follow the steps below.

1. Pick up an item on your partner's desk. Ask what it's called in English.

2. Ask one follow-up question about the item.

3. Change roles. Repeat steps 1 and 2.

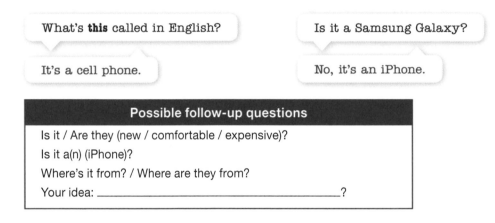

What's **this** called in English?

It's a cell phone.

Is it a Samsung Galaxy?

No, it's an iPhone.

Possible follow-up questions
Is it / Are they (new / comfortable / expensive)?
Is it a(n) (iPhone)?
Where's it from? / Where are they from?
Your idea: _____?

C 🔁 Work with your partner. This time:

1. Point to an item on your partner's desk. Ask what it's called in English.

2. Ask one more question about the item.

3. Change roles. Repeat steps 1 and 2.

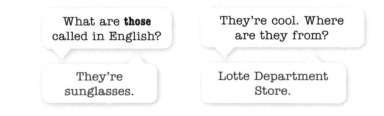

What are **those** called in English?

They're sunglasses.

They're cool. Where are they from?

Lotte Department Store.

D 🔁 Repeat **B** and **C** with a new partner. Use items around the classroom.

WRITING

A Read a rating of this item. Is it a good phone? Why or why not? Tell a partner.

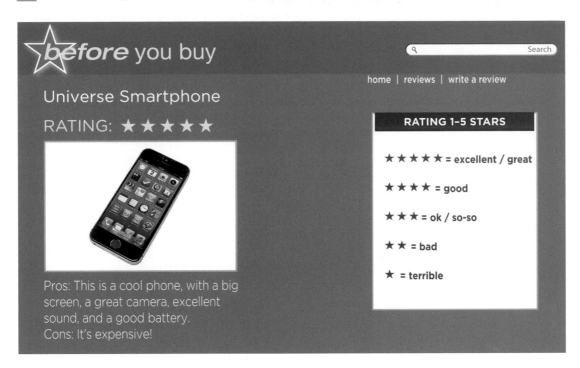

before you buy

Universe Smartphone

RATING: ★ ★ ★ ★ ★

Pros: This is a cool phone, with a big screen, a great camera, excellent sound, and a good battery.
Cons: It's expensive!

home | reviews | write a review

RATING 1–5 STARS

★ ★ ★ ★ ★ = excellent / great

★ ★ ★ ★ = good

★ ★ ★ = ok / so-so

★ ★ = bad

★ = terrible

B Think of a product (a phone, a tablet, a bike, headphones, etc.).

1. What's good about it? Write one or two things. What's bad about it? Write one thing.

2. Find a photo of it online.

6 COMMUNICATION

A Tell four people about your item from above. Show the photo. Then listen and complete the chart below with information about their products.

Product name	Pros	Cons
Example: Universe	The screen is big. The sound is excellent. The battery is good.	It's expensive.
1.		
2.		
3.		
4.		

B Which product from your list in **A** is the best? Why? Tell a new partner.

> The Universe? Oh yeah, that's a good phone.

1 STORYBOARD

A Adriano and Li Mei are students. It's the first day of class. Complete the conversations.

B 👥 In groups of three, practice the conversations.

C 👥 Switch roles and practice the conversations again.

2 SEE IT AND SAY IT

A Look at the picture. Find these things.

a cell phone	a watch	a backpack	keys	a camera
sunglasses	a skateboard	a book	a hat	a person's name

B Talk about the picture with a partner.

- Where are the people?

- Where are they from? Who is / isn't on vacation?

- Point to three things in the picture. Ask and answer:
  What's this / What are these called in English?

- Ask one more question about the picture.

C Choose two people in the picture.
Role-play a short conversation between the people.

> Excuse me? Are these your keys?
>
> Yes, they are. Thanks!

3 COUNTRIES AND NATIONALITIES

A 🔄 Read the clues. Complete the crossword puzzle. Check your answers with a partner.

Across

1. The capital of _____ is Berlin.

4. Beijing is the capital of _____.

6. The Queen of England lives in this city. _____

7. A person from Brazil is _____.

9. The capital of Canada is _____.

10. The _____ Opera House is in Australia.

Down

2. In this country, people speak Spanish. _____

3. Tokyo is the capital of _____.

5. _____ is the capital of South Korea.

7. A person from the United Kingdom is _____.

8. This city is the capital of Italy. _____

4 COME IN TODAY!

A 🔊 Listen to the announcement. Then complete the sentences. **CD 1 Track 25**

1. Everything at Good Buys is on sale for _____.

   a. one day
   b. two days
   c. three days
   d. one week

2. Good Buys is a(n) _____ store.

   a. book
   b. online
   c. clothing
   d. electronics

3. At the sale, you get _____.

   a. a phone for 25 dollars
   b. free headphones
   c. 25 dollars
   d. a free phone

Word Bank
free = costing no money
sale = when an item costs less money

SMALL TOWN, BIG CITY

A Look at the pictures. Use the words in the box and compare the two places. Take turns with a partner.

> The city is big and....
> The town isn't. It's....

beautiful	big	boring	busy	crowded
exciting	fun	interesting	old	relaxing

B Which place do you like—the small town or the big city? Why?

C Tell your partner about a famous town or city. Your partner guesses the city.

> This city is very exciting. It's a big city. It's in Argentina.

> Is it Buenos Aires?

4 ACTIVITIES

A woman looks at her phone
on a crowded subway.

Look at the photo. Answer the questions.

1 Where are the people?

2 What is the woman doing?

3 What are three things you do every day?

UNIT GOALS

1 Describe what you're doing

2 Tell how you are feeling and ask how other people are feeling

3 Talk about school subjects and activities

4 Talk about long-term plans

A group of students sitting outside of a school building

1 VIDEO Day in the Life of a College Student

A ▶ Watch the video with the sound off. Where are these people? What do they do? Write three things.

_____

_____

_____

B ▶ Watch the video again with the sound on. Check your answers.

C ⟳ What are the people in the video doing? Tell a partner.

2 VOCABULARY

A What are these people doing? Match each sentence with a photo.

1. He's **doing** his homework and **studying** for a test.
2. He's **watching** TV.
3. He's **texting** a friend.
4. She's **exercising** and **listening** to music.
5. He's **talking** on the phone.
6. She's **eating** pizza and **drinking** soda.
7. They're **going** to school.
8. She's **shopping**.

B Cover up the sentences. Point to a person and ask your partner a question.

What's he doing?

He's doing his homework.

3 LISTENING

A 🔊 **Pronunciation: Question intonation.** Read the dialog below. Practice it with a partner.

A: How are you[1] doing today?
B: Fine, thanks. How about you[2]?
A: I'm doing great.

[1] Sounds like *How're you*
[2] Sounds like *How 'bout you*

B 🔊 **Pronunciation: Question intonation.** Listen and repeat.
CD 1 Track 26

C 🔊 **Make predictions.** You will hear three conversations in **D**. Read the key words from each conversation. What are the people doing in each situation? Tell a partner what you think.

Conversation 1: *popular, expensive, buy*
Conversation 2: *park, running*
Conversation 3: *notebook, pen*

D 🔊 **Listen for gist and details.** Listen to the conversations. What is each person doing? Circle the correct answer.
CD 1 Track 27

1. A   B   C
2. A   B   C
3. A   B   C

E 🔊 Check your answers with a partner.

4 SPEAKING

A 🔊 👥 Listen to the conversation. Then answer the questions with a partner.
CD 1 Track 28

1. What is Shinja doing? What is Luis doing?

2. How is Shinja? How is Luis?

SHINJA: Hello?

LUIS: Hey, Shinja. It's Luis.

SHINJA: Hi, Luis. How are you doing?

LUIS: Fine. How about you?

SHINJA: So-so.

LUIS: Yeah? What's wrong?

SHINJA: I'm waiting for the bus. It's late!

LUIS: Sorry to hear that.

SHINJA: What are you doing, Luis?

LUIS: Not much. I'm watching TV.

B 👥 Practice the conversation in **A** with a partner.

SPEAKING STRATEGY

C 👥 Complete the dialogs below. Use the Useful Expressions to help you. Then practice the dialogs with a partner.

Useful Expressions
Greeting people and asking how they are

Positive ☺	A: Hi, Sara. How are you doing? B: Fine. / OK. / All right. / Not bad. How about you? A: I'm fine, thanks.
Negative ☹	A: Hi, Yuki. How's it going? B: So-so. / Not so good. A: Really? / Yeah? What's wrong? B: I'm waiting for the bus. It's late!

1. A: Hi, _____. How _____?
   B: _____ good.
   A: Really? _____?
   B: I'm studying for a test. It's hard!

2. A: Hi, _____. How _____?
   B: Fine. How _____?
   A: All _____. What _____?
   B: Not much. I'm reading a book.

D 👥 Ask four people in your class how they are doing today.

5 GRAMMAR

A Turn to page 201. Complete the exercise. Then do **B** and **C** below.

The Present Continuous Tense: Affirmative and Negative Statements				
Subject pronoun	*be*	(*not*)	verb + *-ing*	Contractions with *be*
I	**am**			I am = I'm; I am not = I'm not
You	**are**	(not)	**working.**	you are = you're; you are not = you're not / you aren't
He / She / It	**is**			she is = she's; she is not = she's not / she isn't
We / They	**are**			we are = we're; we are not = we're not / we aren't

B Look at picture A below. What are the people doing? On a piece of paper, write five sentences. Use the present continuous tense.

C 🔁 Work with a partner. Look at pictures A and B. Point to a person and ask a question. Find the differences in the pictures.

> What's he doing?

> In picture A, he's talking on the phone.

> But in picture B, he isn't talking on the phone. He's....

6 COMMUNICATION

A 🔲 Follow the steps below.

1. Get into groups of four. Read the actions. Look up any words you don't know.

dancing to rap music	studying for an exam
exercising at the gym	talking to a boyfriend or girlfriend
playing soccer	texting a friend
playing video games	waiting for the subway
reading a funny book	walking to school
shopping for a graduation gift	watching a sad TV show
sleeping late	working at an office

2. Write each action above on a piece of paper. Mix up the pieces of paper and place them face down.

3. One student takes a piece of paper but doesn't show the others. The student has one minute to act out the action. What is he or she doing? The other three students have one minute to guess by asking *Yes / No* questions. If they guess correctly, the group gets a point.

   > Are you playing soccer?

4. Take turns as the actor and repeat step 3 until you use all the slips of paper. Which group has the most points?

Rules

1. You cannot make any sounds when you are acting out the action.

2. You cannot point to other objects as clues. You *can* point to people if they get part of the answer.

B 🔲 Play the game again. Make slips of paper and use your own ideas.

My name is Luis and I go to Simon Bolivar University in Caracas, Venezuela. I'm studying music with *El Sistema*, a national music program. I'm taking classes like math, science, and history, too. Also, this term, I'm preparing for the college entrance exam.

1 VOCABULARY

i You can also say:
I go to / I'm a student at....
I'm studying / I'm majoring in IT at the *University of Lima.*

A 🔄 Which subjects and majors from the chart do you know? Tell a partner. Add one more idea. Then tell the class.

B 🔄 Read about the student above. Answer the questions with a partner.

1. Where is Luis a student?
2. What is he studying?
3. What classes is he taking?
4. What is he preparing for?

C 🔄 Tell a partner about yourself. Use some or all of the sentences below.

I'm a student at.... / I go to....
I'm majoring in....
I'm taking a... class.

My favorite subjects are....
I'm preparing for the... exam.
I work in....

> I'm taking an art class this term.

School **subjects** and college **majors**
🎨 art
💻 business
⚙️ engineering
🖼️ graphic design
🏛️ history
📡 information technology (IT)
⚖️ law
🧮 math
⊕ nursing
🔬 science
🎒 tourism / hospitality

2 LISTENING

A 🔁 **Make predictions.** What classes are shown by the photos? Tell a partner.

B 🔊 **Distinguish speakers.** What class is each man taking? Match each speaker (1, 2, or 3) with a photo. **CD 1 Track 29**

C 🔊 **Listen for details.** Read the choices below. Then listen again. Circle the <u>two</u> true answers in each sentence. **CD 1 Track 29**

1. He's _____.
   a. a good artist
   b. majoring in art
   c. taking the class for fun

2. He's _____.
   a. working in a hotel
   b. trying to get a better job
   c. taking three classes

3. He's _____.
   a. not having fun in class
   b. preparing for a class
   c. trying to lose weight

D 🔁 Answer the questions with a partner.

1. Point to a picture above. What class is each man taking?
   Why is he taking the class? Use your answers in **B** and **C** to explain.

2. Are you (or someone you know) taking any of these classes? Why?

> He's taking....

> He's trying to....

3 READING

A Look at the photos and captions. Where is Nicolas Ruiz studying this term?

B **Identify main ideas.** Read the interview. Write each question in the correct place to complete it.

Where are you living?

So, are you enjoying Hong Kong?

How's your Chinese?

Which classes are you taking?

So, how's it going?

C **Infer meaning.** Find the words in *italics* below in the reading. Then circle the correct words.

1. A *roommate* is a person you study / live with.

2. If something is *improving*, it is / isn't getting better.

3. *I'm having a great time* means someone is / isn't having fun.

D 🔊 **Find key details.** Read the interview aloud with a partner. Then answer the questions on a piece of paper.

1. What school is Nicolas studying at this term? Why is he going to this school?

2. Where is he living?

3. What classes is he taking?

4. How is he doing in his language class?

5. Is he enjoying Hong Kong? Why or why not?

E 🔊 Imagine you can study in another country. What do you want to learn? Make a new interview with a partner.

> So, Kenji, tell our readers about yourself.

> I'm from Tokyo. This term, I'm studying at the Fashion Institute of Technology in New York.

STUDY ABROAD

People gather in downtown Hong Kong at night.

In this issue of *Study Abroad* magazine, Emma Moore is talking to Nicolas Ruiz, a student from Argentina. He's studying in Hong Kong this term.

Emma: So, Nicolas, tell our readers a little about yourself.

Nicolas: Well, I'm from Argentina. At home, I'm a student at the University of Buenos Aires. This term, I'm studying at the University of Science and Technology, here in Hong Kong.

Emma: Why this school?

Nicolas: Well, I'm majoring in business, and the University of Science and Technology has a great business school.[1]

Emma: 1. _____

Nicolas: Great! The classes are really interesting, and I'm learning a lot. There are also students from all over the world here.

Emma: 2. _____

Nicolas: I'm in a dorm[2] with a roommate. He's from Malaysia and he's really nice.

Emma: Glad to hear it. So, tell us about school. 3. _____

Nicolas: I'm taking three business classes and one Chinese class.

Emma: 4. _____

Nicolas: It's OK. My speaking is improving. Now I can talk to people outside of school.

Emma: Excellent. 5. _____

Nicolas: Oh, yeah. I'm having a great time. There's a lot to do and see. It's a really exciting and beautiful city.

Emma: That's wonderful. Thanks a lot for your time, Nicolas, and good luck with your studies!

[1]At a university, there are many *schools* (the school of business, education, law, etc.). Each school focuses on one area of study.

[2]A *dormitory (dorm)* is a school building where students live.

Hong Kong University of Science and Technology

4 GRAMMAR

A Turn to page 202. Complete the exercises. Then do **B** and **C** below.

The Present Continuous Tense: Extended Time	
Question	**Response**
What **are** you **doing** these days / nowadays?	I'**m studying** in Hong Kong this term.
Are you **enjoying** Hong Kong?	Yes, I'**m having** a great time!

B 🔁 Two old friends meet on the street. Complete the conversation with the present continuous tense. Use the words given. Then practice with a partner.

ZACK: Hey, Leo!

LEO: Hi, Zack!

ZACK: How are you doing?

LEO: I'm all right. How about you?

ZACK: Not bad. So, (1. what / you / do) _____ these days?

LEO: (2. I / study) _____ at State University.

ZACK: Really? (3. What / you / major) _____ in?

LEO: Graphic design. What about you? (4. you / work) _____ or (5. you / go) _____ to school?

ZACK: Both. (6. I / work) _____ part-time at a cafe. (7. I / take) _____ two classes at City College this term, too.

LEO: (8. What / you / study) _____?

ZACK: Photography and art history.

LEO: (9. you / enjoy) _____ the classes?

ZACK: Yeah. They're fun and (10. I / learn) _____ a lot.

C 🔁 Make a new conversation. Use your own information in **B**.

A photographer

5 WRITING

A Complete the interview with your answers.

Studying English: Interview Questions

1. Why are you studying English?

☐ I'm doing it for fun.   ☐ I'm doing it for my job.

☐ I want to travel.   ☐ I'm preparing for an exam.

☐ I'm majoring in English.   ☐ Other: _____

2. What are you learning in your English class these days?

_____

_____

3. How are you doing in your English class? Is your English improving?

_____

_____

4. Outside of class, how are you practicing English?

_____

_____

6 COMMUNICATION

A  Interview three people. Use questions 1–4 in **Writing A**. Write each person's answers on a piece of paper.

Why are you studying English?

Is your English improving?

I'm preparing for the TOEFL.

My speaking is, but my listening....

B Work with a new partner. Tell your partner about the three people you interviewed. Use (but don't read) your notes. Which answers are the most popular in your class?

Juan and Jin Soo are preparing for the TOEFL.

5 FOOD

A spread of food and spices

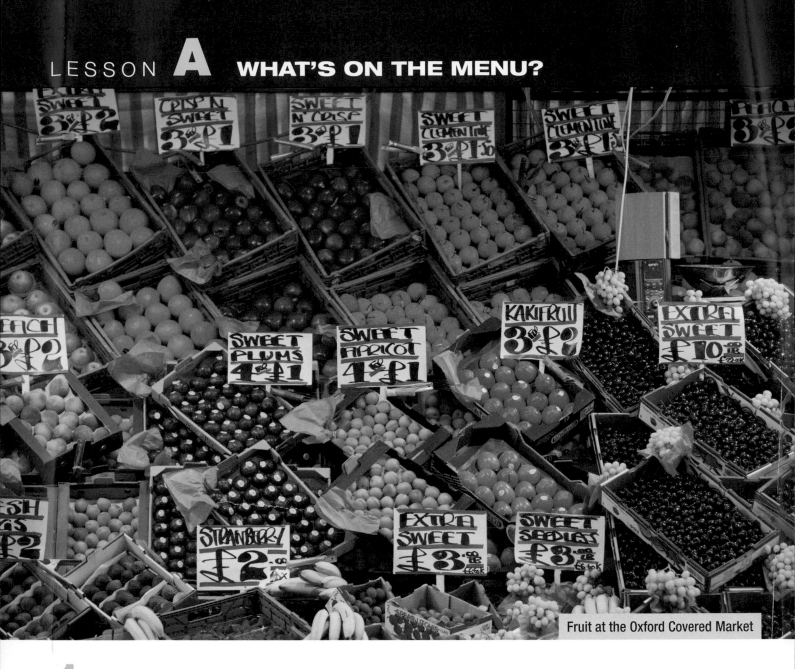

Fruit at the Oxford Covered Market

1 **VIDEO** At the Covered Market

A ▶ 🔁 Watch the video with the sound off. What foods do you see? Tell a partner.

B ▶ Watch the video. Write the food each person doesn't like.

meat	fish	tomatoes

1. Jan _____
2. Richard _____
3. Amy _____

C 🔁 Do you want to go to Oxford Covered Market? Why or why not? Is there a market like Oxford Covered Market where you live? Tell a partner.

2 VOCABULARY

A  With a partner, think of a few fruits and vegetables in English. Do you like to eat any of these items? Share your ideas with the class.

B 🔁 Look at the pictures and the list of drinks. Ask and answer the questions with a partner.

1. Do you ever eat or drink any of these items?
2. Which ones do you like?
3. What other foods and drinks do you like?

steak **and** baked potato

spinach salad **with** tomatoes **and** onions

cheese **and** fruit

spaghetti **and** tomato sauce

vegetable soup **and** bread

rice **and** beans

fried chicken

tuna sandwich

Common drinks
☕ coffee
🥛 milk
🧃 orange juice
🥤 soda
☕ tea

3 LISTENING

A 🔄 What restaurants do you like? What do you order there? Tell a partner.

B 🔊 **Listen for details.** Mia and Leo are at a restaurant for lunch. Listen. Circle the items that they order from the bills to the right. Then answer the questions. **CD 1 Track 31**

1. Which person eats in the restaurant ("for here")?
   _____

2. Which person eats out of the restaurant ("to go")?
   _____

C 🔊 🔄 **Pronunciation: *And, or.*** Listen and complete each conversation with the word *and* or *or*. Notice how *and* and *or* are pronounced. Then practice the conversations with a partner. **CD 1 Track 32**

1. A: Umm... I'd like the spaghetti with tomato sauce.
   B: OK, that comes with soup _____ salad.

2. A: I'd like a chicken sandwich.
   B: OK, that comes with French fries _____ mixed vegetables.

3. A: What juices do you have?
   B: Apple _____ orange.

4. A: Is that for here _____ to go?
   B: For here.

D 🔄 With a partner, order your lunch from the items in **B**. Use the words for ordering food and talking about meals to help you.

Word Bank
Ordering food
What can I get you? / Would you like anything to drink?
I'd like a soup and salad, please. / Orange juice, please.
Talking about meals
breakfast (morning), *lunch* (afternoon), *dinner* (evening)
I <u>have</u> eggs and coffee <u>for</u> breakfast.

Date	Server	For here	Order No
		To go	**0142**

NO		AMOUNT
	MAIN DISHES	
	Chicken sandwich	
	Rice and beans	
	Spaghetti	
	Veggie burger	
	SIDE DISHES	
	Soup	
	Salad	
	French fries	
	Mixed vegetables	
	DRINKS	
	Soda	
	Coffee	
	Bottled water	
	Apple juice	
	Orange juice	
	TAX	

Mia's order

Date	Server	For here	Order No
		To go	**0143**

NO		AMOUNT
	MAIN DISHES	
	Chicken sandwich	
	Rice and beans	
	Spaghetti	
	Veggie burger	
	SIDE DISHES	
	Soup	
	Salad	
	French fries	
	Mixed vegetables	
	DRINKS	
	Soda	
	Coffee	
	Bottled water	
	Apple juice	
	Orange juice	
	TAX	

Leo's order

4 SPEAKING

A 🔊 🔁 Listen to the conversation and practice it with a partner. Then answer the questions. **CD 1 Track 33**

1. What can you eat at Tapeo 39?
2. What is perfect for summer? Why?

JASON: I'm hungry.

MARIA: Me, too. Do you like Indian food?

JASON: No, not really.

MARIA: How about Spanish food? I know a fun place.

JASON: Yeah? What is it?

MARIA: It's called Tapeo 39, and they have great gazpacho there.

JASON: What's gazpacho?

MARIA: It's a delicious kind of soup. I like it a lot.

JASON: It's too hot for soup, Maria!

MARIA: Don't worry. It's a cold soup. It's perfect for summer.

JASON: What's in it?

MARIA: Tomatoes, cucumbers, onions, and pepper.

JASON: Sounds good.

MARIA: It is. Oh, and they also have tasty sandwiches.

JASON: Let's go!

Gazpacho

SPEAKING STRATEGY

B Think of two restaurants. Write the information.

Restaurant name: _____   Restaurant name: _____

Kind of food: _____   Kind of food: _____

Food on the menu: _____   Food on the menu: _____

C 🔁 Make new conversations with your partner. Use the conversation in **A** and your information from **B**, as well as the Useful Expressions, to help you.

Useful Expressions		
Talking about likes and dislikes		
Do you like Indian food? Do you like fish?	Yes! I love it!	😁
	Yes, I like it a lot.	😊
	Yeah, it's OK.	😐
	No, not really.	🙁
	No, I can't stand it.	😫

Hey, Pablo, I'm hungry.

I'm hungry, too. I know a great place for dinner. Do you like Chinese food?

5 GRAMMAR

A Turn to page 203. Complete the exercises. Then do **B** and **C** below.

Simple Present Affirmative Statements		
Subject pronoun	**Verb**	
I / You / We / They	eat	meat.
He / She / It	eats	

Simple Present Negative Statements		
Subject pronoun	***do + not***	**Verb**
I / You / We / They	don't	eat	meat.
He / She / It	doesn't	

B Use the verbs in the box to complete the facts about Sylvie. You will use some words more than once. Check your answers with a partner.

do	drink	eat	go	know	study

Sylvie	You
For breakfast, she…	For breakfast, I…
1. _____ a glass of orange juice. But she (not) _____ coffee. She can't stand it. 2. _____ eggs and toast. They're her favorite.	1. _____ 2. (not) _____ _____
After school, she sometimes…	After school, I sometimes…
3. _____ to a cafe and _____ her homework. 4. _____ with friends in the library. Then they _____ dinner together.	3. _____ and _____ my homework. 4. _____ with friends. Then we _____ together.
Italian food is her favorite. She…	_____ food is my favorite. I…
5. _____ a good place for pizza and pasta. 6. (not) _____ there often. It's expensive.	5. _____ a good place for _____. 6. (not) _____ there often.

C Now complete the information above about yourself. Tell a partner.

6 COMMUNICATION

A You are having a dinner party. Read about your six dinner guests.

Mary

She's from London, England. She plays guitar in a band. She doesn't eat meat. She is Danny's girlfriend.

Lisa

She's from Manila, in the Philippines. She's an actress. She speaks English, Spanish, and Tagalog. She doesn't drink alcohol.

Paula

She's from São Paulo, Brazil. She studies art at the University of London. She likes soccer.

Tomas

He's from the Dominican Republic. He speaks English and Spanish. He loves spicy food. He plays baseball.

Danny

He's from Los Angeles, in the United States. He's an actor. His brother works in South America. He loves Italian food.

Diego

He's from Buenos Aires, Argentina. He lives in Canada now. He teaches music at the University of Toronto.

B Plan the party!

1. With a partner, make a menu for the dinner party.

   Think about your dinner guests' likes and dislikes.

2. Choose a seat at the table for each person. Include yourself and your partner.

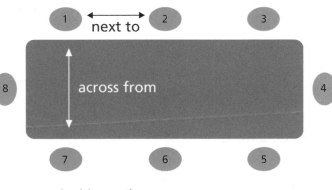

C Get together with a new pair. Explain your menu and table seating.

> Here's our menu. For dinner, we are having....

> Paula is in seat one. She's next to Tomas. They both like sports. She's across from....

Tips for Being a Healthy Eater

DO...

1. eat **healthy** foods, like fruit, when you want a **snack** (a little food between meals). Fruit has **vitamins** like A and C, and these are **good for you**.

2. eat foods like fish, eggs, and yogurt. They give you **energy**, and you can think and work better.

DON'T...

1. eat lots of **junk food** like candy or chips. These things **taste good**, but they have a lot of sugar and salt. Too much is **bad for you**. Soda is high in sugar, too.

2. **skip** breakfast. Eat it every day. This meal gives you energy to start your day.

1 VOCABULARY

A 🔁 Read the tips above. Then answer the questions.

1. To be a healthy eater, what is good to do? What's not good to do? Why?

2. Which tips do you do? Tell a partner.

> I don't eat junk food. I don't like it.

Word Bank
Opposites
good for you ↔ bad for you
healthy ↔ unhealthy
have / eat breakfast ↔ skip breakfast
taste good ↔ taste bad

B 👥 Complete the sentences with a partner. Use new ideas. Then tell another pair.

To be healthy:

1. eat foods high / low in....
2. don't eat.... It tastes good, but it's bad for you.
3. only drink a little.... Too much is bad for you.
4. don't skip....
5. eat.... It gives you energy.
6. eat...for a snack.

C 🔁 Make a poster with a partner using your ideas from **B**. Share your poster with the class and vote for a winner.

2 LISTENING

A 🔊 **Make and check predictions.** The items in the photos are used to make a smoothie. Guess: What is a smoothie? Circle your answer. Then listen to check your answer. **CD 1 Track 34**

a. a soup   b. a drink   c. a main dish   d. a dessert

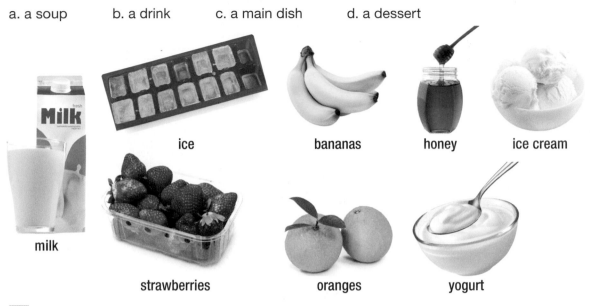

milk   ice   bananas   honey   ice cream

strawberries   oranges   yogurt

B 🔊 **Listen for details.** Listen again. What is <u>not</u> used to make the smoothie? Put an X on it. **CD 1 Track 34**

C 🔊 **Listen for sequence.** How do you make the smoothie? Put the pictures in order from 1 to 7. Then listen and check your answers. **CD1 Track 35**

cut it into pieces

blend everything

peel the fruit

add the other ingredients

put oranges in the blender

put ice in the blender

add the other fruit

D 🔄 Tell a partner how to make a smoothie. Use your answers in **C**.

> To make a smoothie, first you.... Then you....

E 🔄 Do you ever drink smoothies? Are they healthy? What's in them? Tell a partner.

3 READING

A Find the words in *italics* below in your dictionary. Then answer the questions with a partner.

1. Which *illness*—*cancer* or a *cold*—is very bad?

2. Where is your *stomach*? Where is your *skin*? Point to each one.

B **Scan for information.** Read and answer questions 1–3 about your food only.

Student A: Read about chili peppers.

Student B: Read about licorice.

1. Where does the food come from?

2. How do people use it today?

3. Why is it good for us?

C Ask your partner the questions in **B** about his or her food. What are the answers? Take notes.

D **Read for details.** Are statements 1–9 about chilies (C), licorice (L), or both (B)? Write the correct letter.

_____ 1. is / are high in vitamin C

_____ 2. is / are in cold medicine

_____ 3. give(s) you energy

_____ 4. come(s) from Asia and Europe

_____ 5. can help people with cancer

_____ 6. is / are in sweet foods and drinks

_____ 7. make(s) you less hungry

_____ 8. come(s) from the Americas

_____ 9. can stop stomach and skin problems

E Name another healthy food. Answer the questions in **B** about it. Tell a partner.

TWO POWERFUL HEALTH FOODS

Chili peppers are a type of fruit from the Americas. They were first used 6,000 years ago! Today, people all over the world, from Mexico to Thailand, use chilies in their cooking.

Chili peppers taste good, but they're also good for us. They are high in[1] vitamin C. This keeps you healthy. Many chilies are also spicy. This spice gives you energy. It also makes you less hungry, so you eat less. Doctors think chili peppers can stop some kinds of cancer, too.

[1] If something is *high in* vitamin C, it has a lot of vitamin C.

Red chili peppers

Licorice, a type of plant, comes from southern Europe and Asia. Today, when people hear the word *licorice*, they think of candy. In fact, licorice is in some sweet foods (like candy) and drinks (like soda), but it is also a very old medicine.[2] Two thousand years ago, people used licorice for colds and other illnesses. Today, it is still in some cold medicines. People also use it for stomach and skin problems. And now doctors think licorice—like chili peppers—can help people with cancer!

[2] *Medicine* is something you drink or eat to stop an illness.

Red licorice candy has no real licorice in it. Black licorice is much healthier!

4 GRAMMAR

A Turn to page 204. Complete the exercises. Then do **B–D** below.

Simple Present *Yes* / *No* Questions				Short Answers
Do	you	like	spicy food?	Yes, I do. / No, I don't.
	they			Yes, they do. / No, they don't.
Does	he / she			Yes, he / she does. / No, he / she doesn't.

B Read the sentences. Add one more sentence about eating and health.

Find someone who...	Classmate's name
1. has breakfast every day.	
2. drinks two glasses of water every day.	
3. eats a lot of junk food.	
4. drinks soda every day.	
5. likes spicy food.	
6. takes vitamins.	
7. eats a healthy snack every day.	
8. _____ .	

C Use the sentences in **B** to ask your classmates *Yes* / *No* questions. Find a different person for each answer. Write the person's name. The winner is the person to complete the chart first!

> Do you have breakfast every day?

> No, I don't. But I drink three sodas every day.

D Tell a partner about three answers from your chart in **B**.

> That's a lot!

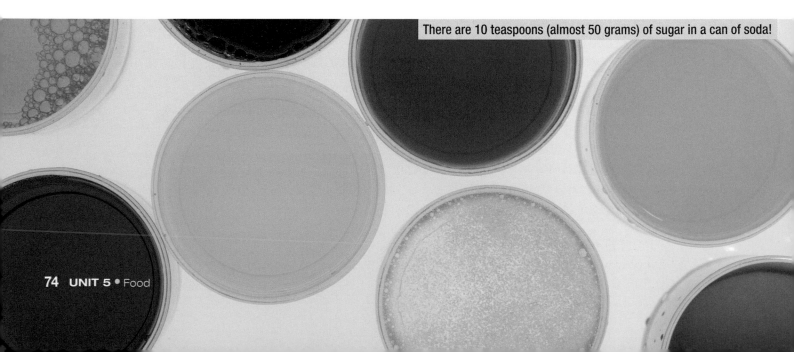

There are 10 teaspoons (almost 50 grams) of sugar in a can of soda!

5 WRITING

A Answer the questions about your favorite food. Write your ideas in a few words.

1. What is your favorite food?

2. Where is it from?

3. What's in it?

4. When do people eat it (for breakfast, lunch, dinner, or as a snack)?

5. Is it good or bad for you? Why?

B Use your notes in **A** to write a paragraph about your food. Use the example to help you.

My favorite dish is paella. It is from Spain. People eat it for lunch. It has rice, chicken, seafood, onions, tomatoes, vegetables, and a spice called saffron. It's delicious and very healthy. It's high in protein, and the vegetables are good for you, too.

6 COMMUNICATION

A Prepare a short talk about your favorite food.

1. Practice: Use your notes from Writing **A** to talk about your food. Do not just read your paragraph.

2. Find a photo, a map, or a video clip to use in your presentation.

B 👥 Work in a group of four. Give your presentation. Then listen to the other members of your group. When you listen, take notes. Answer the questions in Writing **A** about your partners' foods.

C 👥 Your group talked about four foods. Do you like each one? Why or why not? Take turns asking and telling the group.

> Do you like pizza?

> It's okay, but it's not very healthy. Do you like it?

> Yeah, I love it!

6 RELATIONSHIPS

Look at the photo. Answer the questions.

1 Are they a big or small family?

2 How many people are there?

3 What are they doing?

UNIT GOALS

1 Identify and ask questions about family members

2 Describe relationships

3 Ask about a person's age

4 Talk about things you have or own

A man plays music for his family in Mongolia.

The Cason family standing in front of their house.

1 **VIDEO** Megafamily

A 🔁 Look at the picture. What do you think this video is about? Tell a partner.

B ▶ 🔁 Watch the video. Answer the questions. Check your answers with a partner.

1. How many children are in the family? _____

2. How old is the oldest child? _____

3. How old is the youngest child? _____

C 🔁 Do you have a big or small family? How many brothers and sisters do you have? Tell a partner.

2 VOCABULARY

A Find Amy in the chart below. With a partner, use the list to identify her family members.

Amy's family 25 years ago

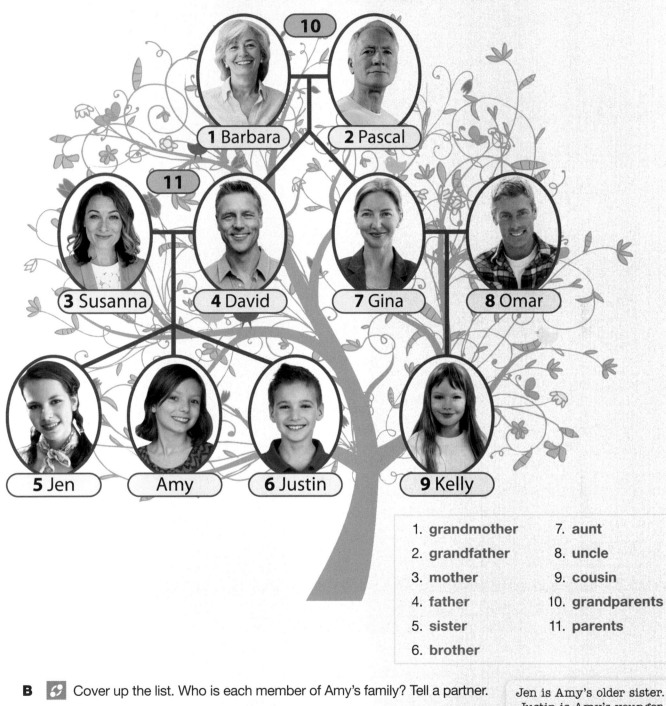

1 Barbara 10 2 Pascal

11 3 Susanna 4 David 7 Gina 8 Omar

5 Jen Amy 6 Justin 9 Kelly

1. **grandmother**	7. **aunt**
2. **grandfather**	8. **uncle**
3. **mother**	9. **cousin**
4. **father**	10. **grandparents**
5. **sister**	11. **parents**
6. **brother**	

B Cover up the list. Who is each member of Amy's family? Tell a partner.

> Jen is Amy's older sister. Justin is Amy's younger brother.
>
> Susanna is Amy's mother.

C Answer these questions with a partner.

1. Amy lives with her parents and grandparents. Who do you live with?

2. Amy is **close to** her grandmother. She loves her grandmother very much, and they talk often. Who are you close to in your family?

3 LISTENING

A **Make predictions.** Here is Amy's family today. Where are they? Look up the captioned words you don't know.

Hi, it's Amy again. This is my family today.

B 🔊 **Listen for details.** Now listen and match each name with the correct person above. **CD 1 Track 37**

a. Amy   c. Sean   e. Erin   g. Justin

b. Tom   d. Gabby   f. Marie

C 🔊 **Listen for details.** Listen again. Match the questions and answers. **CD 1 Track 37**

1. Who is a teacher? _____   Amy
2. Who likes school? _____   Marie
3. Who plays sports? _____   Gabby
4. Who is Tom's mother? _____   Tom
5. Who is a baby? _____   Erin

D 🔄 Sean teaches math. His daughter, Erin, likes math at school. Erin is just like her dad. In your family, who are you like? Tell a partner.

I'm just like my mom. We both love art.

Word Bank
Erin is *just like* her dad.
Erin *takes after* her dad.

4 SPEAKING

A  Listen to the conversation between Beth and Lucas.
Then answer the questions. **CD 1 Track 38**

1. How many brothers and sisters does Lucas have?

2. How many brothers and sisters does Beth have?

BETH: You have a really nice family.

LUCAS: Thanks.

BETH: How many brothers and sisters do you have?

LUCAS: I have two sisters and two brothers. I also
have lots of cousins!

BETH: Wow, you have a big family!

LUCAS: Yes, I do. What about you, Beth? Do you
have any brothers and sisters?

BETH: I have a younger sister.

LUCAS: Are you close?

BETH: Yes, we are. We talk about everything.

Useful Expressions	
Asking and answering questions about family	
How many people are (there) in your family?	(There are) four: me, my brother, and my parents.
Do you have any brothers and sisters?	Yes, I have a sister. / No, I'm an only child.
Are you close (to your sister)?	Yes, I am. / No, not really.

B Practice the conversation in **A** with a partner.

C Use the Useful Expressions to ask three classmates about their families.

Classmate's Name	Family	Brothers and Sisters	Close to...

D Tell a new partner about the people in your chart.

> Ruben has a big family. He's close to his sister, Isabel.

5 GRAMMAR

A Turn to page 205. Complete the exercises. Then do **B–F** below.

Possessive Nouns			
Singular nouns	**Plural nouns**	**Irregular plural nouns**	**Proper nouns**
sister → sister**'s**	brothers → brother**s'**	children → children**'s**	Derek → Derek**'s**

B 🔊 ⟳ **Pronunciation: Possessive 's.** Listen and repeat. Then practice saying the expressions with a partner. **CD 1 Track 39**

my <u>sister's</u> son   his <u>wife's</u> name   <u>Lucas's</u> family

the <u>boy's</u> name   <u>Beth's</u> friend   Mr. <u>Gomez's</u> children

your <u>mom's</u> friend

C ⟳ Look again at the family tree on page 79. Ask and answer the questions below with a partner.

1. How many people are in Amy's family tree?

2. How many people are in her immediate* family?

3. What are her parents' names?

4. What is her brother's name?

5. What is her sister's name?

6. What are her grandparents' names?

7. What is her cousin's name?

8. What is her aunt's name?

9. What is her uncle's name?

*immediate family = parents, children, and close relatives who live in the same home

D Now draw your family tree on a piece of paper. Don't label any of the people.

E ⟳ Take turns asking a partner about his or her family tree. Use questions like the ones in **C**.

> What are your grandparents' names?

F ⟳ Using the answers in **E**, fill in the family tree with your partner's information.

The British Royal Family *from left* front: Charles and Camilla; back: William, Kate, Harry

6 COMMUNICATION

A 🔁 Look at this photo of a famous family. What do you know about them? Tell a partner.

B Complete the sentences below about the family in **A**. Check your answers at the bottom of the page.

1. William is Kate's _____.
2. Kate is William's _____.
3. William and Harry are _____.
4. Charles is William and Harry's _____. William and Harry are his _____.
5. Camilla is William and Harry's stepmother. Do you know their mother's name? _____

C 🔁 Research a famous person's family with a partner. Answer the questions. Find photos of the famous person and his or her family.

1. What is the famous person's name?
2. What is the person's job?
3. Who are four or five people in the person's family? What are their names? How are they related?
4. Are they also famous?
5. What is one interesting thing about this family?

D 👥 Get together with another pair.

1. Introduce your person and show a photo. Ask: Do you know anything about this person's family?
2. With your partner, talk about the person's family. Show photos. The other pair will listen and take notes.

> This is Angelina Jolie's family. Her husband is Brad Pitt. Angelina and Brad are famous actors.

> They have six children. This is her son Maddox. He's from Cambodia. He's adopted.

E 👥 What does the other pair remember about your family? Ask them four questions to check.

> Who is Angelina's son from Cambodia?

1. husband 2. wife 3. married 4. father, sons 5. Diana

1 VOCABULARY

Kimora's family

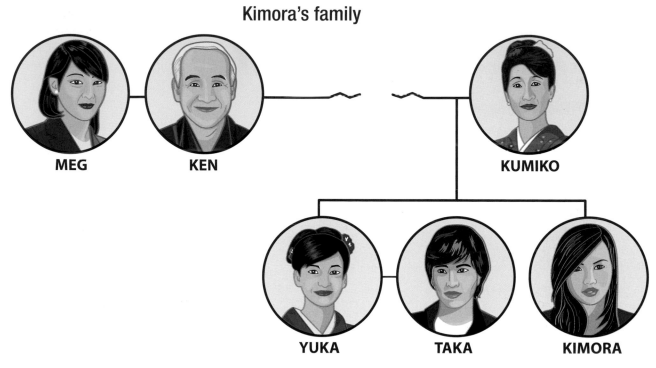

MEG   KEN   KUMIKO

YUKA   TAKA   KIMORA

- My parents, Ken and Kumiko, are **divorced**. My dad remarried. His wife's name is Meg.

- My mom isn't married, but she isn't single either. She's **dating someone**. His name is Haru.

- My older sister, Yuka, is **married**. Her husband's name is Taka.

- And me? I'm **single**. I'm really busy with school. I don't have time for a **boyfriend**.

A Work with a partner. Ask and answer the questions about Kimora's family.

Who…

1. is married?
2. is single?
3. is divorced?
4. has a boyfriend?
5. is Kimora's stepmother?
6. is Ken's ex?

Word Bank
Talking about relationships
I'm **dating someone**. My **boyfriend's** / **girlfriend's** name is….
I'm **single**. I'm not dating anyone right now.
She's **married**. Her husband's name is….
He's **divorced**. But he and his **ex**-wife are friends.

B Talk with a partner about three people. They can be family members, friends, or famous people. Are they married, single, divorced, or dating someone?

2 LISTENING

A 🔄 Think of a famous person. Ask a partner about the person's age.

> How old is Lionel Messi?

> He's twenty-nine or thirty, I think.

B 🔄 Look at the chart. What does it show? Tell a partner.

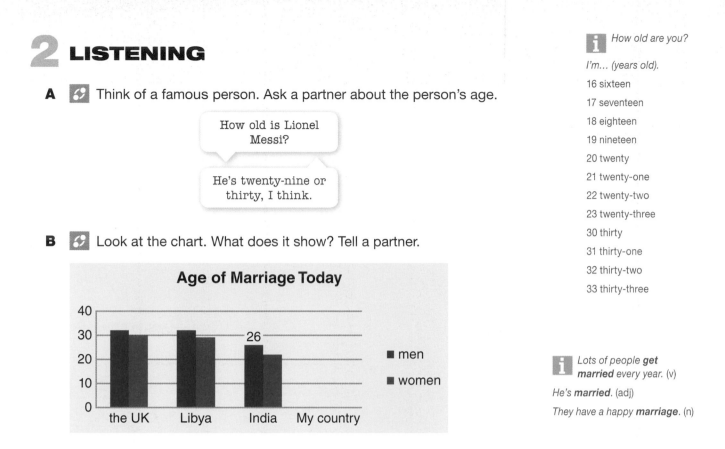

Age of Marriage Today

■ men
■ women

the UK   Libya   India   My country

26

i *How old are you?*
I'm... (years old).
16 sixteen
17 seventeen
18 eighteen
19 nineteen
20 twenty
21 twenty-one
22 twenty-two
23 twenty-three
30 thirty
31 thirty-one
32 thirty-two
33 thirty-three

i *Lots of people **get married** every year.* (v)
*He's **married**.* (adj)
*They have a happy **marriage**.* (n)

C 🔊 **Listen for gist.** Listen to the first part of an interview. Complete the sentence with the correct answer. **CD 1 Track 40**

In some countries, more people are getting married _____ these days.

a. younger   b. later

D 🔊 **Listen for details.** Listen to the full interview. Write the ages above the bars in **B**. **CD 1 Track 41**

E 🔄 Add ages for your country in **B**. Look online. Is your country similar to the other countries? Tell a partner.

A wedding in Mexico

3 READING

A  **Make predictions.** Today, many people marry later or not at all. Why? Tell a partner.

B **Read for details.** Read the passage. Then match the statements (a–f) with each person. Two answers are used twice.

Mei Li _____

Wei _____

a. is dating someone now.

b. has an apartment.

c. 's parents want him or her to marry soon.

d. is single.

e. wants to marry but can't.

f. has a job.

C With a partner, make a short dialog. Use ideas from the reading. Then say your dialog for another pair.

Student A: You're Mei Li's or Wei Yang's parent. You want your child to marry soon. Why?

Student B: You're Mei Li or Wei Yang. You aren't married. Why? Tell your mom or dad.

> Mei Li, you're 28. It's time to get married.

> Dad, I like my freedom. I've got a good job and....

> Yes, but single life isn't easy.

D Answer the questions. Compare your ideas with a partner.

1. Who do you agree with: Mei Li or her parents?

2. In your country, are weddings expensive? Who pays?

TIME TO GET MARRIED?

Mei Li Zhao, 28, lives in Chengdu, China. She's got a good job, a nice apartment, and lots of friends. "I've got a great life," says Ms. Zhao. But her parents don't agree. Mei Li is single and they are worried. "You're twenty-eight years old," they say. "It's time to get married."

Mei Li isn't alone. Today in China, more women and men get married in their thirties[1]. But some parents, like Mei Li's, worry about this. In some places in China, it's common[2] for a woman to marry by age 27 or 28. Mei Li understands her parents, but she's not ready for marriage. "Right now," she says, "I like my freedom.[3]"

Wei Yang, 31, lives and works in Beijing. He is also not married. "I've got a girlfriend," he says, "but I can't get married now." Why? In many large cities—like Beijing, Shanghai, and Hong Kong—life is very expensive. A wedding can cost $15,000 or more, and a man's family pays for it. Wei Yang has a job and some money, but not enough for a wedding. "Everyone tells me 'It's time to get married,'" he says, "but today, it's not so easy."

[1]If you are *in your thirties*, you are between the ages of 30–39.
[2]If something is *common*, it is something most people do or think.
[3]If you have a lot of *freedom*, you can do anything you want.

A man and woman in China take wedding photos.

 **GRAMMAR**

A Turn to page 206. Complete the exercises. Then do **B–D** below.

Have got			
I**'ve** / You**'ve** / We**'ve** / They**'ve**	got	a big family. a nice apartment. a lot of free time. black hair.	I**'ve got** = I **have got** He**'s got** = He **has got**
He**'s** / She**'s**			

B Circle the things in the box that you have. Then compare answers with a partner.

a boyfriend or girlfriend	a brother or sister	a car	a big family
a phone	a pet	a son or daughter	a job

A: Which things do you have?

B: I've got a younger brother. What about you?

A: I've got a younger brother, too. He's 15. How old is your brother?

B: He's 16.

C Which things do you and your partner both have?
Tell another pair.

> We've both got younger brothers.
> Her brother is 15. My brother is 16.

D Which things does everyone in your group have?
Tell the class.

> We've all got brothers, but they're
> different ages. Lena's brother is 15.
> My brother is....

Are there any **twins** in your class?

88 UNIT 6 • Relationships

5 WRITING

A 🔁 Read about Dmitry's family. Then do the following:

   1. Find and correct six mistakes with apostrophes.

   2. Tell a partner: Who does he live with? Does he have any brothers or sisters? Are they married?

> My name is Dmitry, and I'm 21 years old. I live with my parent's in Moscow. I've got an older sister. Shes 29 and married, and shes got a one-year-old daughter. Her babys name is Olga. My sister lives in Kiev with her husband. He's got a big family, and theyre very close. In fact, his mother lives with my sister and her husband. My sister and her husband both work. His mom watches Olga. Its a big help.

B Answer these questions. Take notes.

   1. What's your name? How old are you?

   2. Who do you live with?

   3. Do you have any brothers or sisters? Do you have a favorite aunt, uncle, or cousin?

   4. How old are they? Are they married? Do they have children? Where do they live?

Use an apostrophe (') to...
1. join two words (*I have got = I've got, she is = she's*)
2. show possession (*Dmitry's family, my parents' house*)

C Use your notes in **B** to write a paragraph about your family. Use the sample to help you.

D 🔁 Exchange papers with a partner.

   1. Answer questions 1–4 in **B** about your partner.

   2. Correct any mistakes.

   3. Give the paper back to your partner.

   4. Make corrections to your paragraph.

6 COMMUNICATION

A Take the survey. Mark your top three answers.

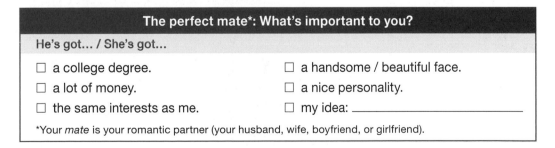

The perfect mate*: What's important to you?
He's got... / She's got...
☐ a college degree.   ☐ a handsome / beautiful face.
☐ a lot of money.   ☐ a nice personality.
☐ the same interests as me.   ☐ my idea: _____
*Your *mate* is your romantic partner (your husband, wife, boyfriend, or girlfriend).

B 👥 Work in a small group. Tell them your answers. Explain your reasons.

> For me, the perfect mate has got....

C 👥 Now answer these questions together.

   1. Are men's and women's answers similar or different?

   2. What answers from **A** are the most common in your group? Tell the class.

1 STORYBOARD

A Tony and Paloma are in a cafe. Complete the conversation.

B 🔁 Practice the conversation with a partner.

C 🔁 Change roles and practice the conversation again.

2 SEE IT AND SAY IT

A Look at the picture of the food court. Answer the questions.

1. What food and drinks are healthy?
2. What food and drinks are unhealthy?
3. What food and drinks do you like?
4. Look at the people. What are they doing?

B Imagine you are in the food court. Follow the directions.

1. Choose a place and order some food.

> **Student A:** You are the server. Ask your partner for his or her order.
>
> **Student B:** Order something to eat and drink.

2. Change roles and repeat step 1.

C Think of a new restaurant for the food court. Answer the questions.

1. What kind of restaurant is it (Korean, Italian, Mexican, etc.)?
2. What is your new restaurant called? Give it a name.
3. What food and drinks are on the menu? Make a list.

D Share your ideas in **C** with another pair.

3 ODD WORD OUT

A  Look at the groups of words. Circle the one that's different in each group. Tell your partner.

> In number 1, *teacher* is different.

1. mother	father	(teacher)	daughter
2. study	go to school	do homework	get married
3. math	test	business	nursing
4. sausage	breakfast	lunch	dinner
5. rice	soup	meal	chicken
6. mother	sister	aunt	nephew
7. listening to	studying for	majoring in	preparing for
8. bad for you	high in sugar	unhealthy	tastes good

4 HE SPEAKS SPANISH

A  Look at the picture. What things does this person have in his backpack? Tell a partner.

> He's got a dictionary in his backpack.

B What do you know about this person from the things in his backpack? Make sentences. Use the verbs in parentheses.

1. (be) _His name is Brian Hughes_____.
2. (speak) _____.
3. (be) _____.
4. (go) _____.
5. (like) _____.
6. (play) _____.
7. (have) _____.
8. (study) _____.

C  Take four or five things from your backpack or purse and put them on your desk. Then look at your partner's things. What do you know about your partner from his or her things? Ask your partner questions.

> You have keys. Do you drive?

> No, I don't. These are my house keys.

NUMBERS GAME

1. Write numbers between 11 and 100 in your BINGO chart.

2. When you hear a number that's in your chart, write an *X* over it.

3. When all your numbers have an *X*, say *Bingo!* Be the first person, and you are the winner!

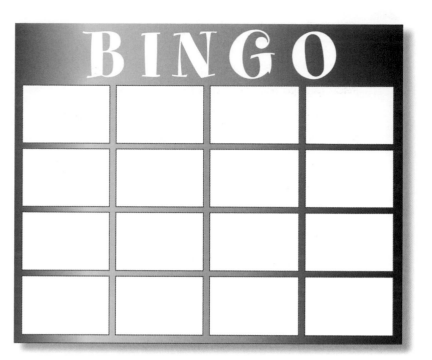

 ## WHAT'S WRONG?

A Are these sentences true or false? Write *T* or *F*. Correct the underlined words and numbers to make the false sentences true.

+	plus
–	minus
=	equals

_____ 1. Your father's sister is your <u>cousin</u>.

_____ 2. 37 + 22 = <u>sixty</u>.

_____ 3. Your father's sister is your <u>aunt</u>.

_____ 4. Your uncle's son is your <u>sister</u>.

_____ 5. 100 – 24 = <u>seventy-six</u>.

_____ 6. Your aunt's son is your <u>nephew</u>.

_____ 7. Here is a pattern: three, six, nine, twelve, <u>fourteen</u>, eighteen, twenty-one, twenty-four.

_____ 8. Your parents are divorced. Your father marries again. His new wife is your <u>stepmother</u>.

B Check your answers at the bottom of the page. You get one point for each correct answer. How many points do you have?

1. F; aunt, 2. F; 59, 3. T, 4. F; cousin, 5. T, 6. F; cousin 7. F; fifteen, 8. T

The astronomical clock in Prague, Czech Republic

Look at the photo. Answer the questions.

1 Look at the clock in your classroom. How do you say these times in English?

   12:00   12:30

2 Here are the days of the week:

Sunday	**Thursday**
Monday	**Friday**
Tuesday	**Saturday**
Wednesday	

Which one is your favorite?

3 When is the weekend in your country? Say the day(s).

UNIT GOALS

1 Describe your daily routine

2 Make suggestions about activities and plans

3 Identify the time of day or week

4 Ask and answer questions about weekend activities

People rush through a busy train station in Germany.

1 **VIDEO** Late for Work

A Before you watch, do this:

1. Look up the word *late* in your dictionary.
2. Look at the pictures and the vocabulary on page 97.

B  The man in the video starts work at 9:00. Watch the first 30 seconds. Circle your answer.
The man is / isn't late for work.

C ▶ Watch the entire video. What does the man do in the video? Put the events in order from 1 to 7.

_____ He washes his face.　　　 _____ He reads a text message.　　　 _____ He gets dressed.

_____ He wakes up.　　　 _____ He has breakfast.　　　 _____ He leaves home.

_____ He brushes his teeth.

D ⟳ Answer the questions with a partner.

1. Look at the sentence in **B** again. Is the man late for work? How do you know?
2. Does this ever happen to you?

2 VOCABULARY

A  Study the times below. Then cover up the words and take turns telling the time with a partner.

What time is it?

It's....

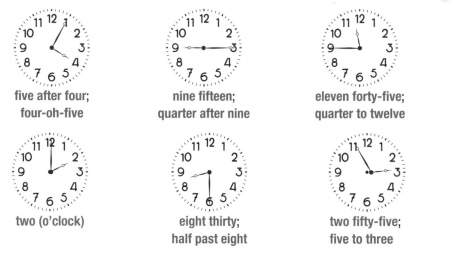

five after four;
four-oh-five

nine fifteen;
quarter after nine

eleven forty-five;
quarter to twelve

two (o'clock)

eight thirty;
half past eight

two fifty-five;
five to three

B Practice telling the times shown below with a partner. Then read about Hiro's daily routine.

He wakes up at 7:30
and has breakfast.

Then he takes a shower
and gets dressed.

8:20

He leaves home at 8:20
and goes to school.

9:00

His classes start at 9:00 and
finish at 4:00.

4:50

At 4:50, he studies English.

5:45

After that, he goes home
at 5:45.

12:00

He eats dinner at 8:00. He
goes to bed at midnight.

C Use the words in **B** to tell your partner about your daily routine.

I wake up at 5:30.

That's early!

3 LISTENING

A 🔄 Look at the words *yesterday*, *today*, and *tomorrow* in the box. Then complete the sentences. Compare answers with a partner.

If today is Friday, then tomorrow is _____. Yesterday was _____.

B 🔊 **Listen for gist.** Pilar and Alma are talking about Pilar's plans for today and tomorrow. Write *today* or *tomorrow* for each activity. **CD 2 Track 2**

1. go to school _____
2. have a piano lesson _____
3. see a movie _____
4. study English _____
5. take a swimming class _____
6. take a test _____

C 🔊 **Listen for details.** Write your *today* answers from **B** on lines 1–4 below. When does Pilar plan to do each of these activities? Listen again and write the start and finish times. **CD 2 Track 2**

Activity	Start Time	Finish Time
1. _____	_____	_____
2. _____	_____	_____
3. _____	_____	_____
4. _____	_____	_____

D 🔄 Tell a partner about Pilar's day.   Pilar goes to school at....

E 🔊 **Pronunciation: Numbers.** Listen and repeat. Notice the different stress. **CD 2 Track 3**

13 / 30   14 / 40   15 / 50   16 / 60   17 / 70   18 / 80   19 / 90

F 🔊 **Pronunciation: Numbers.** Listen to the sentences. Circle the correct answer. **CD 2 Track 4**

1. I wake up at 6:14 / 6:40 every morning.
2. The train to school takes about 19 / 90 minutes.
3. She drives 17 / 70 kilometers to work.
4. After dinner, I study for an hour and 15 / 50 minutes.
5. It's his birthday today. He's 16 / 60 years old.

G 🔊 🔄 **Pronunciation: Numbers.** Listen again and check your answers. Take turns saying the sentences in **F** with a partner. **CD 2 Track 4**

4 SPEAKING

A 🔊 💬 Listen to the conversation. Then complete the sentences with a partner. Circle the correct answer. **CD 2 Track 5**

It's noon.
It's midnight.

1. Adriano   Jessie   Both   …want(s) to eat French food tonight.
2. Adriano   Jessie   Both   …want(s) to see the new superhero movie.
3. Adriano   Jessie   Both   …want(s) to see the James Bond movie.

ADRIANO: What do you want to do tonight, Jessie?

JESSIE: I don't know. Hey, let's have dinner at that new French restaurant.

ADRIANO: Hmmm… I don't really like French food. And I'm not very hungry.

JESSIE: OK, well, we could see a movie.

ADRIANO: Yeah, that sounds good. Let's see the new superhero movie.

JESSIE: Hmmm… I don't really want to see that. What else is playing?

ADRIANO: Well, the new James Bond movie is at the AMC Theater.

JESSIE: Great idea. When is it playing?

ADRIANO: At 8:15.

JESSIE: At 8:50?

ADRIANO: No, *8:15*. And there's a late show at midnight.

JESSIE: Midnight is late! Let's go to the 8:15 show.

ADRIANO: OK!

B 💬 Practice the conversation with a partner.

SPEAKING STRATEGY

C 💬 Use the Useful Expressions to complete the dialogs. Then practice with a partner.

1. A: What do you want for lunch?
   B: _____ Mexican food.
   A: _____. I love Mexican food!

2. A: What do you want to do after class?
   B: _____ play video games.
   A: _____ video games.
   B: OK, well, _____ see a movie.
   A: _____. What do you want to see?

Useful Expressions
Making suggestions

Making a suggestion
Let's see a movie.
We could see a movie.
Saying *yes*
(That) sounds good.
Good / Great idea.
Saying *no* politely
I don't really like French food.
I don't really want to see that movie.

D 💬 Add three or four more lines to dialog 2 in **C**.

Student B: Suggest a movie to see.

Student A: You don't want to see Student B's movie. Suggest another idea.

Students A & B: Agree on a movie and a time to see it.

5 GRAMMAR

A Turn to page 207. Complete the exercises. Then do **B–D** below.

Prepositions of Time	
When is your class?	It's **on** Monday(s). / It's **on** Tuesday night.
	It's **in** the morning / afternoon / evening. It's **at** night.
	It's **at** 8:30 / noon.
	It's **from** 4:00 **to** 5:30. / It's **from** Tuesday **to** Saturday.

B ⟳ Complete the answer choices with *in*, *at*, *on*, *from*, or *to*. Then choose the answers that are true for you.

People study at the library at Colegio de San Nicolas in San Michoacan, Mexico.

1. When do you like to study?

   a. _____ the morning

   b. _____ the afternoon

   c. _____ the evening

   d. late _____ night

2. When do you do most of your homework?

   a. _____ weekdays

   b. _____ Saturdays and Sundays

   c. both

3. What day is your birthday this year?

   a. It's _____ Monday.

   b. It's _____ Tuesday.

   c. It's _____ Wednesday.

   d. other: _____

4. You can see a movie with your friends _____ noon or _____ midnight.

   Which do you choose? _____

5. What is your favorite subject at school? What time does the class meet?

   My favorite subject is _____.

   The class is ____ _____ from _____ ____ _____.
   　　　　　　　(day(s) of the week)　　　(start time)　　(end time)

C ⟳ Now interview a partner. Use the questions in **B**. Take notes.

D ⟳ What is one new thing you know about your partner now? Tell him or her.

> You do your homework on weekdays and Saturdays and Sundays. I think you're a serious student.

6 COMMUNICATION

A Read the directions below.

1. At the top of the schedule, write today's day (Monday, Tuesday, etc.) and the next two days.

2. Complete the calendar with your schedule for these three days (school, work, English or music lessons, an appointment, seeing friends, etc.). You can also add new ideas. Write the activities next to the times in the calendar. If you have no plans, leave the time blank.

9:00 AM			
10:00 AM			
11:00 AM			
NOON			
1:00 PM			
2:00 PM			
3:00 PM			
4:00 PM			
5:00 PM			
6:00 PM			
7:00 PM			

B Work with a partner. Read the example. Then find time in both your schedules to do the three activities together.

- practice English   • see a movie   • your idea: _____

A: Let's study together for the test. Are you free today at 1:00?

B: No, sorry, I'm busy. Are you free tomorrow?

A: Well, I have classes from 11:00 to 4:00, but then I'm free.

B: OK, let's meet at 4:15.

A: That sounds good!

People at a party in Amsterdam.

1 VOCABULARY

A 🔄 Look at the photo. Where are these people? Do you ever do this on the weekend with your friends? Tell a partner.

B Look at the activities with *go* in the Word Bank and read sentences 1–4. Then complete 5–10.

On the weekend, I usually...

1. ___go for a walk___ . (a walk)
2. ___go dancing___ . (dance)
3. ___go to a party___ . (a party)
4. ___go out with friends___ . (with friends)
5. _____ . (the movies)
6. _____ . (a bike ride)
7. _____ . (shop)
8. _____ . (a friend's house)
9. _____ . (with my family)
10. _____ . (the gym)

Word Bank
Activities with *go*
go + -ing verb **go dancing**
go to + a place **go to a party / the beach**
go for + an activity **go for a walk**
go out + with + someone **go out with friends**

C In **B**, check (✓) the activities you do on the weekend.

D 🔄 Compare your answers with a partner's. Are your weekends similar or different? Do you do other activities?

2 LISTENING

A Read the sentences. Then tell a partner: Is a *day off* a free day or a workday?

Tomorrow is my <u>day off</u>. I don't work or go to school.

B **Listen for details.** Nick and Kelly are talking. Listen. Check (✓) the days Nick works. Put an X on his day(s) off. **CD 2 Track 6**

☐ Monday

☐ Friday

☐ Saturday

☐ Sunday

C **Listen for details.** What is good and bad about Nick's day(s) off? Listen. Write one word in each blank. **CD 2 Track 7**

Good: Most people are at work or _____. Most places aren't _____.

Bad: Nick's friends are _____. He does most things _____.

D **Listen for details.** Listen again. Check (✓) the things Nick does on his day off. **CD 2 Track 7**

☐ He goes shopping.   ☐ He goes for a bike ride.

☐ He goes to the movies.   ☐ He wakes up late.

☐ He does homework.   ☐ He goes out with friends.

E Is your day off similar to or different from Nick's? Why? Tell a partner.

3 READING

A  Look at the pictures in the reading. What are the people doing? Tell a partner.

B **Make predictions.** Match a person (1, 2, 3, or 4) with one or more activities (a–f) below.

Person

1. The Couch Potato _____
2. The Workaholic _____
3. The Party Animal _____
4. The Health Nut _____

Activity

a. likes to exercise

b. wakes up late on the weekend

c. goes out all night

d. doesn't like to go out on weekends

e. is always thinking about work or school

f. wakes up early

C **Check predictions; Read for specific information.** Now read the article. Check your answers in **B**.

D Work in a group of 3–4 people. Answer the questions.

1. What kind of weekend person are you? Why? Which type is most common in your group?

2. Think of something you want to do this weekend. Suggest it to your partners. Can you all agree?

3. What kind of weekend person is your best friend?

THE HEALTH NUT

For you, the weekend isn't a time to relax; you want to go out and do things! You usually wake up early (yes, even on the weekend) and go for a walk, a run, or a bike ride. All week, you're inside at school or work. On the weekend, it's time to go outside and be active!

WHAT KIND
OF WEEKEND PERSON
ARE YOU?

For many people, the weekend is a time to relax and have fun. But not everyone has fun in the same way. Here's how different people spend their weekends. What type of person are you?

THE COUCH POTATO

What's your perfect weekend? Sleeping late, watching TV, and playing video games. Sure, you like to spend time with[1] friends—but only at home.

[1] If you *spend time with* people, you do something together.

THE WORKAHOLIC

It's the weekend and it's time to relax… but not for you. The Workaholic is always busy: working, studying, talking on the phone, texting classmates, or checking emails. When you go out with friends on the weekend, you're thinking about your homework or your next exam.

THE PARTY ANIMAL

For you, the weekend is all about fun—and lots of it. Your night starts at 9:00 or 10:00. You go dancing or to a party with friends. Later, you go home and sleep all day. Then you wake up in the afternoon and do it all again!

4 GRAMMAR

A Turn to page 207. Complete the exercises. Then do **B** and **C** below.

Simple Present *Wh-* Questions				
Question word	*do / does*	Subject	Verb	Answers
Who	do	you	study with?	(I study with) Maria.
What	does	she	do on Saturdays?	(She) goes out with friends.
When	do	they	have class?	(They have class) at 9:00.
		we		(We have class) on Mondays.
Where	does	he		(He has class) in Room 3B.

B 🔁 Read about Zoe's weekend. Unscramble questions 1–4. Start each sentence with a question word. Then ask and answer the questions with a partner.

On Saturday, Zoe...	On Sunday, Zoe...
• works at a department store from 9:00 AM to 3:30 PM. • goes to the gym in the afternoon. • goes out with friends at night.	• wakes up at 11:00 AM. • goes for a bike ride in the afternoon. • studies in the evening.

1. Zoe / what / do / on Saturday afternoon / does

   _____? *She goes to the gym* _____.

2. she / work / does / when

   _____? _____.

3. does / work / she / where

   _____? _____.

4. who / on Saturday night / Zoe / does / go out with

   _____? _____.

C 🔁 Write four more questions about Zoe's schedule. Use different question words. Then ask and answer the questions with a partner.

1. _____

2. _____

3. _____

4. _____

> What time does Zoe get up on Sunday?

5 WRITING

A  Read the texts between Raquel and her friends, Monika and Alex. Answer the questions with a partner.

1. What does Raquel suggest?

2. Who says *yes*? What does the person suggest?

3. What do these symbols mean in the texts?

☹   ♥   👍

B Write a text to a partner. Suggest something to do tonight or this weekend. Say when and where it is.

C Exchange texts with your partner. Read his or her message. Then write a text back saying *yes* or *no*. If you say *no*, give a reason.

D Repeat **B** and **C** with a new partner.

6 COMMUNICATION

A Read the questions on the left side of the chart. In the *Me* column, check (✓) the activities you do.

Do you...	Me	Classmates	Question	Details
watch TV?			What... ?	
go shopping?			Where... ?	
wake up late?			When... ?	
go out with friends?			Where... ?	
do homework?			What... ?	
spend time with family?			Who... ?	
your idea: _____			_____	

B Interview your classmates. For each question, find a different person to answer *yes*. Write the classmate's name. Ask another question to get more details.

> Do you watch TV on the weekend?
>
> Yes, I do.

> What do you watch?
>
> On Sunday night, I watch....

C Read your notes. What is the most interesting answer? Tell the class.

8 SPECIAL OCCASIONS

Three young women are dressed up for Day of the Dead in Mexico.

Look at the photo. Answer the questions.

1 Where is this festival and when does it happen?

2 Special occasions happen in different seasons. The seasons are:

winter   spring   summer   fall

Which season is your favorite?

3 Here are some more seasons. Which ones happen where you live?

rainy season   dry season

hurricane / typhoon season

UNIT GOALS

1 Talk about important dates

2 Express degrees of certainty

3 Describe when special occasions happen and how they are celebrated

4 Describe what happens at a festival

Instruments at the Ice Music Festival

1 **VIDEO** Ice Music

A Look at the photo above. This video is about "ice music." What do you think ice music is?

B ▶ Watch the video. Circle the correct answer(s).

1. This happens in Norway / Iceland.

2. They make / play ice instruments.

3. They make / cut the ice.

C 🔁 Do you like this music? Tell a partner.

D 🔁 With a partner, plan a music festival. Write down where it takes place, what instruments there are, and who goes. Share your ideas with the class.

2 VOCABULARY

A  Practice saying the months of the year with a partner.

January	
February	
March	
April	
May	
June	
July	
August	
September	
October	
November	
December	

B  Work with a partner.

- Name as many holidays as you can.
- Write each one next to the correct month.
- In two minutes, try to fill up the chart.

C Tell another pair about your list. Which holiday is your favorite?

> In our list, we have Loy Krathong for November.

Loy Krathong Festival, Thailand

3 LISTENING

A 🔊 🔄 **Pronunciation: *th* and *t*.** Practice saying these ordinal numbers with a partner. Then listen and repeat. **CD 2 Track 9**

1st	first	6th	sixth	11th	eleventh	30th	thirtieth
2nd	second	7th	seventh	12th	twelfth	40th	fortieth
3rd	third	8th	eighth	13th	thirteenth	50th	fiftieth
4th	fourth	9th	ninth	↓		↓	
5th	fifth	10th	tenth	20th	twentieth	100th	one hundredth

B 🔄 A student is flying home for summer vacation. Look at the plane ticket below. Then answer the questions with a partner.

1. Where is the person going?

2. How much is the ticket?

Deluxe Airlines

Flight

Traveler's Name:			**Adult**	**Fare** $621.00
	first	last		

from Vancouver, Canada **to** Mexico City, Mexico
   1   2

Depart: ☐   ☐

Return: ☐   ☐

C 🔊 **Listen for numbers and dates.** Listen and complete the information on the ticket with the man's name. What day is he departing? What day is he returning? Write your answers under *1*. **CD 2 Track 10**

D 🔊 **Listen for numbers and dates.** The man changes his travel dates. Listen and write the new dates under *2*. Cross out the old fare and write the new one. **CD 2 Track 11**

E 🔄 Look at the travel dates in **D**. Answer these questions with a partner.

1. Are these good dates to travel in your country?

2. What are the best months for traveling in your country?

Vancouver, Canada

4 SPEAKING

A 🔊 Kendrick and Tanya are studying in the United States. Listen to their conversation. Then answer the questions. **CD 2 Track 12**

1. What holiday is on the first Monday in September in the United States?

2. What do people do on this day? Does Tanya know?

TANYA: So, Kendrick... do you have plans for Labor Day?

KENDRICK: Labor Day?

TANYA: Yeah, it's a holiday here in the US. We have the day off from school.

KENDRICK: Really? When is it?

TANYA: It's on the first Monday in September.

KENDRICK: Sounds good. So, do people do anything special?

TANYA: I'm not sure. It's a long weekend, so some people travel. My host family plans to have a barbecue.

B Practice the conversation in **A** with a partner.

SPEAKING STRATEGY

C Answer the questions with a partner. Use the Useful Expressions to help you.

Useful Expressions		
Saying you know or don't know something		
Is tomorrow a holiday?		When is Labor Day?
Yes, it is. / No, it isn't.	certain	It's on September 3rd this year.
I'm not sure. It could be.	not sure	I'm not sure. Is it in September?
I don't (really) know.	don't know	I don't (really) know.

Speaking Tip

Follow-up questions:

I'm not sure. Is it in September?

I don't know. What do you think?

1. When is Mexico's Independence Day?
   a. May 5th
   b. August 24th
   c. September 16th

2. Where is the New Year called *Hogmanay*?
   a. in Russia
   b. in Scotland
   c. in Iceland

   Where is the New Year called Hogmanay?

3. Where does Children's Day happen on May 5th?
   a. in Italy and Greece
   b. in Chile and Peru
   c. in Korea and Japan

4. What holiday is on October 31st in the United States?
   a. Halloween
   b. Thanksgiving
   c. Christmas

   I don't really know. What do you think?

D Check your answers on page 218. Who has the most correct answers in your class?

A Turn to page 208. Complete the exercise. Then do **B–D** below.

Prepositions of Time: *in* and *on*	
When is the holiday party?	It's **on** December 20th. / It's **on** Christmas Eve. / It's **on** Monday.
	It's **in** December. / It's **in** the winter. / It's **in** (early / late) 2016.

B Study the grammar chart. Then follow the steps below.

spring   summer   fall / autumn winter

1. **Student A:** Read the items in Group 1 aloud to Student B. Write the answers Student B gives.

2. **Student B:** Close your book and listen to your partner. Say the correct preposition for each item. Answer as quickly as you can.

3. Switch roles and repeat with the items in Group 2.

> OK, let's start. Number one. 2002.

> **In** 2002!

Group 1	Group 2
1. _____ 2002	1. _____ May
2. _____ the third Tuesday of the month	2. _____ December 31st
3. _____ March	3. _____ the first Saturday of the month
4. _____ New Year's Day	4. _____ the nineties
5. _____ the spring	5. _____ 2004
6. _____ January 1st	6. _____ the summer
7. _____ the eighties	7. _____ Labor Day

C Complete as much information as you can about your own birthdate.

Your special day

> **i** A *decade* is a period of ten years. For the decade of the 1990s you can say *(in) the nineteen nineties* or just *(in) the nineties.*

1. date (e.g., the 17th)		1. _____
2. month		2. _____
3. year		3. _____
4. decade	of your birth	4. _____
5. season		5. _____
6. day of the week		6. _____
7. time of day*		7. _____

*morning, afternoon, or evening

D Interview a partner about his or her birthdate. Are you similar in any way?

> What is the month of your birth?

> I was born in November.

6 COMMUNICATION

A 🔁 On some holidays or special days, there are expressions people say. Look at the examples in the box. Then do the following:

- What holidays, or special days, are in the photos below? Tell a partner.

- Match an expression in the box with a photo. Write the letter of the expression on the photo.

- Take turns with a partner saying the expression in English for each holiday or special day.

- In your country, what do people say on these days? Tell your partner.

a. Happy Birthday!

b. Congratulations!

c. Happy New Year!

d. Happy Mother's Day.

e. I love you. / Happy Valentine's Day.

> On New Year's Day, people in my country say....

B Answer the questions.

1. What is your favorite day of the year? _____

2. When is it? _____

3. What do you eat or drink on this day? _____

4. What do you do or where do you go? _____

C 👥 Get into a group of four. Share your answers from **B**. Which day of the year is the most popular?

The Highland Games **take place annually** (every year) in the spring and fall all over Scotland.

What happens at the festival:

- People wear **traditional** clothes and play traditional sports. One popular **event** is the hammer throw.
- There are bagpipe **parades**.
- People from around the world **perform** traditional Scottish dances. They **compete** to be the best.
- Thousands of people **attend** the games. People also **celebrate** the games in countries like Brazil and New Zealand.
- Don't **miss** the festival, and **take** lots of **photos**!

Women do a traditional Scottish dance.

A man competes in the hammer throwing event.

1 VOCABULARY

A 🔁 Read about the Highland Games. Look up any words you don't know. Then ask and answer the questions with a partner.

Word Bank
Saying how often something happens
daily, weekly, monthly, annually every two / three / four years

1. Where are the games? _____
2. How often do they take place? _____
3. When do they take place? _____
4. How many people attend? _____
5. What happens at the games? _____
6. Is this event interesting to you? Why? _____

B 🔁 Think of another sporting event or sports festival. Answer questions 1–6 in **A** about it. Tell a partner about the event or festival.

People at Oktoberfest in Munich

2 LISTENING

Word Bank

Types of festivals

art, film, food, holiday, music, sports, spring / summer / autumn / winter

A **Infer information.** Look at the photo. Then answer the questions with a partner.

1. Do you know anything about this festival?
2. Guess: What kind of festival is it?

B **Listen for details.** Read the sentences. Then listen. Circle the correct words. **CD 2 Track 13**

1. Both festivals are spring / summer / winter / autumn festivals.
2. Oktoberfest is a(n) art / food / film / music festival.
3. The Moon Festival is an important art / family / film / sports event.

C **Listen for details.** Read the sentences. Then listen again. Write one word or number in each blank. **CD 2 Track 13**

	Oktoberfest	The Moon Festival
Where does it take place?	in Munich, _____	in _____
When is it?	for _____ days in late _____ or early _____	in late _____ or early _____
What do people do?	eat _____ German food	spend time with _____, eat moon _____, and _____ with colorful lanterns
What other countries have this festival?	_____ and _____	Vietnam and Singapore

D Choose one festival. Tell your partner about it. Use your notes.

> The Moon Festival takes place in....

E Are there autumn festivals in your country? Are they similar to Oktoberfest or the Moon Festival? Tell a partner.

A 🔁 **Infer information.** Look at the photo on the next page with a partner. Guess: Where are the people? What kind of festival is Burning Man?

B 🔁 **Scan for information.** Look quickly at the article. Find answers to the questions. Then ask and answer the questions with a partner.

1. How many people attend Burning Man? _____

2. Where does it take place? _____

3. When is it? _____

4. How long is it? _____

5. What type of festival is it? _____

6. What happens at the end? _____

C **Read for details.** Read the passage closely. Check (✓) the things you can do at Burning Man. Put an X next to the things you cannot do.

_____ play music related to the theme

_____ share things

_____ ride a bicycle

_____ sell clothes

_____ buy food

_____ see interesting art

D 🔁 **Exemplify.** Sit back-to-back with a partner. Imagine you are at Burning Man. Call your partner on the phone. Talk about the festival: What do you see? What are you doing? Is it fun?

E 🔁 Do you think Burning Man is an interesting festival? Why or why not? Is there a similar festival in your country? Tell a partner.

BURNING MAN

Every year, over 60,000 people from all over the world attend the Burning Man festival in the Black Rock Desert in the US. The eight-day event starts on the last Monday in August and ends on the first Monday in September, which is Labor Day in the US.

Every year, Burning Man has a different theme. Some past themes are Time, Good and Bad, The Body, and Hope and Fear. People make art, play music, and wear clothes related to the theme. There are also many activities for people to do—all related to the theme.

The Burning Man festival is very large—about one-and-a-half miles (almost 2.5 km). Many people use a bike to go from place to place. Also, festival-goers cannot buy anything at Burning Man, except some drinks (like water, coffee, and tea) and ice. For this reason, people bring their own food and drinks. They also share things with others.

On the last day, a large statue of a man is burned. It marks the end of summer and the Burning Man festival.

People watch the Burning Man statue burn at the end of the festival.

4 GRAMMAR

A Turn to page 209. Complete the exercises. Then do **B–D** below.

When and How long Questions		
With be	**When** is the festival?	It's **in** July / **on** Thursday. It starts **on** July 1 / **at** 10:00.
	How long is the festival?	(It's) **from** July 1 **to** July 3. (It lasts) **until** July 3 / **for** three days.
With other verbs	**When** do you study?	(I study) **on** Saturdays / **in** the evening.
	How long do you study?	(I study) **from** 4:00 to 6:00 / **until** 6:00 / **for** an hour.

B 🔗 Complete the dialog with *When, How long,* or a preposition. Then practice in pairs.

A: _____ does your vacation start?

B: _____ Friday.

A: _____ is your break?

B: It lasts _____ two weeks, _____ July 3 _____ July 17.

A: So, do you have any plans?

B: Yeah. I'm going to Comic-Con in San Diego, California.

A: Cool! _____ do you leave?

B: _____ July 6.

A: _____ are you in the US?

B: I stay _____ July 13. I return home _____ the 14th.

A: Sounds good. So, _____ is the flight from Lima to San Diego?

B: Nine hours!

C 🔗 Think of a festival to go to. Make a new dialog with a partner.

D 👥 Say your dialog for another pair. When you listen to the other pair, answer questions 1–4.

1. How long is the speaker's break?

2. Where is he or she going?

3. When does he or she leave?

4. How long does he or she stay at the festival?

Over 100,000 people attend Comic-Con International every year. At the event, you can learn about new comic books and science fiction movies and TV shows.

Student Shorts

HOME | ABOUT US | DIRECTIONS | CONTACT US

▶ GUESTS:
Who's Attending

Emma Shea | Jose Alonso | Noah Kim

The 3rd Annual Student Shorts
Film Festival ▶

Time:
Saturday and Sunday
May 8 & 9 | 6:00–11:00 PM

Location:
City College Student Union

More info:
Do you make YouTube videos? Enter your short video and you can win $1,000! Then come and see this year's best videos. Meet the student filmmakers and some famous YouTubers, too. Don't miss it!

This event is free for all students with ID.

5 WRITING

A Read the festival event page. Answer the questions with a partner.

1. What kind of festival is it?
2. What is the festival's name?
3. When and for how long is the festival?
4. Where does it take place?
5. What activities can you do at the festival?
6. Is the event free?

B Think of a festival with your partner. It can be a real one or you can create a new one. Answer questions 1–6 in **A** about it. Then create an event page for it like the one above.

C Give your event page to another pair. Read theirs. Answer the questions.

1. Does their event page answer questions 1–6 in **A**?
2. Are there any mistakes in the writing? If there are, correct them.
3. Can you make their event page better? Say one idea. Then return their page to them.

6 COMMUNICATION

A Get together with a new pair. Show them your event page and tell them about your festival. Repeat this step with five or six pairs in your class.

B Which festival is your favorite? Why? Complete the sentence below and tell the class. Which festivals are popular?

I plan to attend _____.

9 COME TOGETHER

Look at the photo. Answer the questions.

1 How do these people know each other?

2 How do you think these people feel?

3 How often do you think they spend time together?

UNIT GOALS

1 Identify everyday household chores

2 Apologize and respond to an apology

3 Explain how often you do things

4 Ask and answer questions about dating

A couple lies down for a wedding photograph outside of Delhi, India.

Central Park in New York is popular for dates and as a place for friends and family to spend time together.

1 **VIDEO** Instant Date

A ▶ 🔄 A man and woman are sitting in the park. Watch the video with the sound off. Then answer the questions with a partner.

1. How do the man and woman know each other?

2. There is a big surprise. What is it?

B ▶ Now watch the video with the sound on. Put the steps in order. Number them 1–5.

____ a man brings them a drink

____ people play music

____ a man takes their tickets

____ a man brings them food

____ a man gives them tickets

C 🔄 Look at the events in **B**. Where do they usually take place? Tell a partner.

D 🔄 Improv Everywhere is a group in New York City that specializes in pranks (jokes) to bring people together. Do you see pranks in your city or town? Tell a partner.

2 VOCABULARY

A Rina is from Japan. She's a student in Canada. She's living with a host family. Read about her life with her host family. Look up any words you don't know.

Rules for **doing** the family **chores** and **housework**	
Host family	**Student**
The host family gives sheets, towels, a desk, and a bed to Rina.	Rina **makes her bed, cleans her room**, and **empties the trash**.
Rina's host parents **make breakfast** and **dinner** for the family.	Rina eats lunch at school every day. She also **makes a snack** at home.
Rina's host parents **do the grocery shopping** for the family.	Rina helps after dinner. Sometimes she **washes the dishes**.
The host family has a laundry room.	Rina **does her own laundry**.

Rina also helps take care of the family's children.

B Cover up **A**. Complete the sentences with the correct verb. Then decide whether the sentence is *true* or *false*.

1. Rina ___buys___ her own sheets and towels.   True   False
2. Rina _____ her own laundry.   True   False
3. Rina _____ her own grocery shopping.   True   False
4. Rina _____ her own room.   True   False
5. Rina _____ her own breakfast every day.   True   False
6. Rina _____ her own bed.   True   False

Word Bank

Word Partnerships

make breakfast / the bed / a snack

do chores / laundry / the grocery shopping

C 🔁 Check your answers with a partner.

D 🔁 Discuss these questions with a partner.

1. Is Rina's life with her host family similar to your life?
2. Which chores do you do at home?
3. Who does most of the housework?

3 LISTENING

A  **Infer information.** Read about a housework study. Then answer the questions with a partner.

1. Who does more housework?

2. In some countries, men and women *share the chores 50/50.* What does that mean?

3. Where do men and women share the chores 50/50?

B 🔊 **Listen for opinions.** Match each opinion with a person: Paul (P), Junko (J) or Mario (M). One opinion is extra. **CD 2 Track 15**

1. A husband and wife should share the housework. _____

2. Marriage changes people. _____

3. Women are good at housework. Men aren't. _____

4. Women stay at home more. The housework is their job. _____

C 🔊 **Listen for details.** Read the information in the chart. Then listen and check (✓) the correct answer(s) for each person. **CD 2 Track 15**

	is married	has a job	shares the housework 50/50
Paul	☐	☐	☐
Junko	☐	☐	☐
Mario	☐	☐	☐

D 🔊 **Pronunciation: Sentence stress.** Read the sentences. Then listen and repeat. **CD 2 Track 16**

Married men do <u>thirty</u> percent of the housework.

Women do <u>seventy</u> percent.

E 🔊 **Pronunciation: Sentence stress.** Listen and underline the stressed word in each sentence. **CD 2 Track 17**

1. A husband and wife should share the housework.

2. Marriage changes people.

3. I'm calling about the housework study.

4. It's important to share the housework.

5. What do you think?

F  Which of the opinions in **E** (1, 2, or 4) do you agree with? Why? Discuss with a partner. Do you know anyone like Paul, Junko, or Mario?

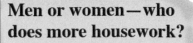

Men or women—who does more housework?

AP—June 7 A study of 17,000 people in 28 countries says married men do 30% of the housework. Women do 70%. Only men and women in Finland, Sweden, and Norway share the chores 50/50.

i 50/50 is pronounced *fifty-fifty.*

Word Bank
take out the garbage = move trash outside to be taken away

Who does more chores in your country, men or women?

4 SPEAKING

A 🔊 Emilio and Adam are university students. They share an apartment. Listen to their conversation and answer the questions. **CD 2 Track 18**

- Adam apologizes (says he is sorry). Why? Underline his apology.

- How does Emilio respond to the apology?

EMILIO: Hey, Adam. I'm home.

ADAM: Hey, Emilio. You're back from your trip already?

EMILIO: Yeah. How are you doing, Adam?

ADAM: Um... fine. How about you?

EMILIO: Great! I... uh... Wow, this room is a mess!

ADAM: Well, I had a party yesterday. Sorry about that.

EMILIO: Don't worry about it, Adam. You never have parties. Come on, let's clean up.

ADAM: No, I can do it.

EMILIO: Hey, I hope it was a fun party.

ADAM: It was!

ℹ️ If a room is a *mess*, it is very dirty.

B 🔄 Practice the conversation with a partner.

SPEAKING STRATEGY

C 🔄 Complete the dialogs. Then practice them with a partner.

1. A: Oh no! I forgot my book.
   B: That's _____. You can borrow mine.

2. A: I'm late for class. _____, Ms. Williams.
   B: Don't _____. We're just starting.

3. A: I didn't make dinner. _____.
   B: No _____. Let's make it together.

D 👥 Choose one of the ideas below. Make a short dialog with your partner. Then say your dialog to another pair.

- You are eating lunch with a friend. The bill comes, but you don't have money to pay.

- Today is your mother's or father's birthday. You don't have a gift.

Useful Expressions
Apologizing
Making an apology
(I'm) sorry.
(I'm) sorry about that.
I'm really sorry. [stronger]
Responding to an apology
Don't worry (about it).
That's OK / all right.
No problem.
Speaking Tip
You can also respond to an apology by saying *Apology accepted*.

5 GRAMMAR

A Turn to page 210. Complete the exercises. Then do **B–D** below.

B Read about Jackie. Then circle the correct answer in sentences 1–3.

Jackie <u>is</u> **sometimes** messy.

Jackie **always** <u>does</u> her grocery shopping on the weekend.

Jackie <u>doesn't</u> **usually** <u>make</u> her bed in the morning.

1. Frequency adverbs come before / after the verb *be*.

2. Frequency adverbs come before / after other verbs.

3. Most frequency adverbs come before / after *not*.

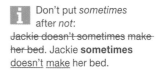

Frequency Adverbs	
always	100%
usually	
often	
sometimes	
hardly ever	
never	0%

i Don't put *sometimes* after *not*: Jackie doesn't sometimes make her bed. Jackie **sometimes** <u>doesn't</u> <u>make</u> her bed.

C Linda and Amy are roommates. Sometimes they have problems. Write each sentence with the frequency adverb given.

Linda says:	**Amy says:**
1. Amy washes her dishes. (hardly ever)	1. Linda is watching TV. (always)
_____	_____
2. She empties the trash. (never)	2. She has loud parties. (sometimes)
_____	_____
3. She makes snacks late at night. (usually)	3. She does her laundry. (hardly ever)
_____	_____
4. She doesn't help around the apartment. (often)	4. She's on the phone late at night. (often)
_____	_____
5. She eats my food. (sometimes)	5. She doesn't clean her room. (sometimes)
_____	_____

D 🔁 Work with a partner. Use the sentences in **C**. One person is Linda; the other is Amy. Talk about your problems. Can you make things better?

> Amy, you hardly ever wash your dishes. It's a mess.

> I'm busy studying for exams. I'm sorry about that, Linda.

6 COMMUNICATION

A Imagine you are a student in an English-speaking country. You are looking for a roommate to share your apartment. Read the questions below. In your answers, use frequency adverbs.

ROOMMATE QUESTIONS	My answer	Partner 1: _____	Partner 2: _____	Partner 3: _____
1. Do you clean your room?				
2. After you cook, do you do the dishes?				
3. Do you study in your own room?				
4. Do you get up and go to bed early?				
5. Do your friends come over and hang out?				
6. Do you have parties?				
7. Your question: _____				

B Use the questions in **A** to interview three classmates.

Do you get up and go to bed early?

Usually, but I like to sleep late on Sunday mornings.

C Think about your three interviews. Who is the best roommate for you? Why? Tell a new partner.

Maria is the best roommate for me. We're very similar. For example...

1. I like a girl and she likes me. But she's my ex-girlfriend's friend. Is it OK to go on a date with her?

2. I'm dating a nice guy. Everyone says we're a good couple. The problem? I don't love him. What can I do?

3. I'm single. I want to meet someone special, but it's hard. What can I do?

1 VOCABULARY

A 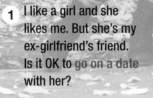 Read the questions above. With a partner, match a question (1–3) with an answer (a–c) below.

_____ a. **Hang out** with other single friends. Try to meet someone this way.

_____ b. Is your ex OK with it? Ask her first. Then you can **ask** her friend on a **date**.

_____ c. It's time to **break up**. Be nice, but end the relationship.

Word Bank

A *date* is a meeting between two people, usually a romantic one.

If you *date* someone, the person is your boyfriend or girlfriend.

Word Bank

verb + *date*	*go on* a date
	invite / ask
	someone on
	a date
adj + *date*	*first date*

B  Answer the questions with a partner.

1. Do you agree or disagree with the advice in **A**?

2. What other ways are there to meet people for friendship? For dating?

3. Do any of your friends date someone? Do you ever hang out with this couple?

> My friend Yoon dates a girl named Hee Jin. I hang out with them sometimes.

4. Imagine you can go on a date with anyone. Finish this sentence:

    I would ask _____ on a date.

2 LISTENING

A  Below are some ways for single people to meet each other. Rank them from 1 (most popular) to 6 (least popular). Then compare answers with a partner.

at school _____

through family members _____

online _____

a blind date _____

at work _____

through friends _____

B 🔊 **Listen for details.** Megan and Connie are talking. Listen and circle the correct answers. **CD 2 Track 19**

1. Seth was Connie's friend / boyfriend.

2. Connie is / isn't dating Seth now.

3. Connie wants / doesn't want to date someone new.

C 🔊 **Listen for a speaker's attitude; Listen for details.** Megan gives Connie some dating advice. Which idea(s) does Connie like? Listen and circle + for like and – for dislike. Then circle the words to complete the sentences. **CD 2 Track 20**

Ways to meet people	Connie's opinion		Reason
1. at school	+	–	Connie wants / doesn't want to see her boyfriend every day.
2. on blind dates	+	–	She wants / doesn't want to know a person first.
3. online	+	–	She wants / doesn't want to try something new.

D  Do you agree with Connie's opinions? Tell a partner.

3 READING

A  **Understand the main idea.**
Read the title of the passage. Q & A means "question and answer." Then read the two questions in **bold**, and the names at the top of the next page. Answer the questions with a partner.

1. What is the reading mainly about?
2. Where are the students from?

B **Read for details.** Read the answers to the first question. Do teenagers date in their countries? Circle *Yes* or *No*. If they say an age, write it.

In Ho   Yes   No   Age: _____

Erin   Yes   No   Age: _____

Valentina   Yes   No   Age: _____

Niels   Yes   No   Age: _____

C **Read for opinions.** Read the entire passage. Then answer the questions. Write the person's name. Sometimes, more than one name is possible.

Who thinks…

1. most teenagers don't have time to date? _____

2. going out in a group is a good way to meet people?

_____

3. most teenage couples break up?

_____

4. a woman can ask a guy on a date?

_____

5. a man should ask a woman on a date? _____

D  Do you agree or disagree with the opinions in **C**? Tell a partner.

> I agree with number 3. Most teenage couples break up.

DATING Q & A
WITH STUDENTS AROUND THE WORLD

The men

In Ho, 22, South Korea
Niels, 20, Holland

Do teenagers date in your country?

In Ho: They usually don't, not in high school. Students are studying a lot and preparing for the college entrance exam. Most people go on a first date later, usually in college.

Erin: People here start dating at 14 or 15. But these couples usually break up after graduation.

Valentina: My parents are strict,[1] so I didn't date in high school. But some people do, at age 16 or so.[2]

Niels: Teenagers date in Holland, but it's very relaxed. Guys and girls often hang out together in groups. This is true even in college and later. It's a good way to meet people.

In Ho: I agree. I often go out with my classmates—both men and women. We go to a club or something like that.

The women

Valentina, 21, Colombia
Erin, 19, New Zealand

Imagine you like someone. Do you invite the person to go on a date with you?

In Ho: Sure. I text the person. If she agrees, we go to a movie or something.

Valentina: I never ask the guy. He should invite me.

Erin: But sometimes a guy is shy.[3]

Niels: Or you like him, but he doesn't know.

Erin: Exactly. So it's OK for a girl to invite the guy, I think.

Niels: I agree.

[1] A *strict* person controls another person, usually with many rules.
[2] *Or so* means about or around.
[3] A *shy* person is quiet and uncomfortable with others.

4 GRAMMAR

A Turn to page 211. Complete the exercises. Then do **B** and **C** below.

Review: Simple Present *Wh-* Questions				
Question word	*do / does*	Subject	Verb	Answers
What	do	you	do on the weekend?	(I / We) hang out with friends.
Where		they	go on dates?	(They usually go to) the movies.

B Work in a group of three. Do the following:

1. Cover Ms. Right's dating profile.

2. Each person then takes one man's profile (Mr. X, Y, or Z). Give your man a name. Then complete his profile with your own ideas. Use a separate piece of paper if needed.

The Dating Game: Who's the best couple?		
Mr. X's name: _____	**Mr. Y's name:** _____	**Mr. Z's name:** _____
Age: _____	Age: _____	Age: _____
Goes to school: Yes / No If yes, where? _____ If no, what does he do? _____	Goes to school: Yes / No If yes, where? _____ If no, what does he do? _____	Goes to school: Yes / No If yes, where? _____ If no, what does he do? _____
Lives where / with who? _____	Lives where / with who? _____	Lives where / with who? _____
Weekend interests? _____	Weekend interests? _____	Weekend interests? _____
Has a car: Yes / No If yes, what kind? _____	Has a car: Yes / No If yes, what kind? _____	Has a car: Yes / No If yes, what kind? _____

C Now read Ms. Right's profile. Find the best match for her. Ask *Wh-* questions about your two partners. Fill in the chart for each man. Who is the best match for Ms. Right?

Ms. Right wants to meet someone who…

- is 20–30 years old
- has his own place
- has a college degree
- has a car
- likes hiking, hanging out with friends, and going to concerts on the weekend

My guy's name is Nico and he's 20.

Where does he live?

5 WRITING

A Look at the question in the box to the right. Then read one person's opinion. Answer the questions below with a partner.

Where is a good place for a first date?

a coffee shop

a club

a movie

a park

a restaurant

My idea: _____

1. Where is the perfect place for a first date?

2. What are the two reasons?

3. Do you agree?

> **In my opinion**, Common Grounds coffee shop on La Playa Avenue is a good place for a first date for two reasons. **For one thing**, it's a nice place but it's not expensive. You can hang out for a long time, and it doesn't cost a lot of money. **Also**, it's very romantic. It's close to the beach and you can see the water. Later, you can go for a walk. **For these two reasons**, Common Grounds coffee shop is a good place for a first date.

B Write a short paragraph. Use the outline to get started.

i Look at the words in **bold** in the sample. These words are used to give an opinion, or explain why you think or believe something.

> In my opinion, ... is the perfect place for a first date.
> For one thing...
> Also...
> For these reasons, ... is a good place for a first date.

C Exchange your writing with a partner.

1. Answer questions 1 and 2 in **A**. Underline the answers in your partner's paragraph.

2. Answer question 3 by telling your partner your opinion.

6 COMMUNICATION

A Work in a small group. Ask the question below about the places in **Writing**. Each person in the group explains their answers. Who thinks... is a good place for a first date?

> Who thinks a coffee shop is a good place for a first date?

> I do. A coffee shop is cheap. It's perfect for students.

> I don't. Coffee shops are always crowded and noisy.

B Which place is most popular? Tell the class.

Els Quatre Gats cafe, Barcelona, Spain

1 STORYBOARD

A Alexis and Peter are at a movie theater. Complete the conversation.

B Get into a group of three. Practice the conversation.

C Change roles and practice the conversation again.

2 SEE IT AND SAY IT

A 🔁 Talk about the photo with a partner.

1. What's the date?

2. What holiday is it?

3. What time is it in the photo? What's happening in the photo?

4. On this holiday, what do you usually do?

B ⚡ Two people at this party are on a date. With a partner, create a dialog between the two people. Role-play your conversation for the class.

3 LISTENING: PHONE MESSAGES

A 🔊 You have four voicemail messages on your phone. Listen. You will hear part of each message. Write the day and date of each call. **CD 2 Track 22**

New Voicemail

🔊

4 missed calls

Message 1 — From: Jack

Day / date of call: _____

Message: There's a good _____ playing at the Strand Theater at _____ .

Message 2 — From: Dr. Miller's office

Day / date of call: _____

Message: You have an appointment at _____ on _____ .

Message 3 — From: Your sister

Day / date of call: _____

Message: I have a _____ tonight. Can you _____ the dishes and _____ the garbage for me?

Message 4 — From: Richard

Day / date of call: _____

Message: I'm calling about lunch _____ . Let's meet at _____ .

B Look at the messages in **A**. Can you guess any of the answers? Tell a partner your ideas.

C 🔊 Listen and complete each phone message in **A**. **CD 2 Track 23**

D Read your messages. What are the problems with the schedule?

4 WEEKEND ACTIVITIES

A Complete each sentence with your information.

On the weekend, I...

always	usually	often	sometimes	hardly ever	never	
☐	☐	☐	☐	☐	☐	wake up early.
☐	☐	☐	☐	☐	☐	go shopping.
☐	☐	☐	☐	☐	☐	go out with friends.
☐	☐	☐	☐	☐	☐	clean my room.
☐	☐	☐	☐	☐	☐	go on a date.
☐	☐	☐	☐	☐	☐	practice my English.

B  Compare your answers with a partner's. Ask and answer questions. Are you similar or different?

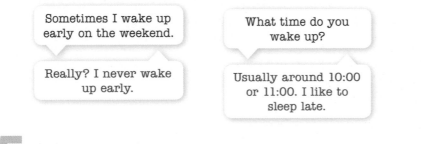

> Sometimes I wake up early on the weekend.

> Really? I never wake up early.

> What time do you wake up?

> Usually around 10:00 or 11:00. I like to sleep late.

5 PARTY INVITATION

A Look at the invitation below. Then make your own party invitation on a piece of paper. Leave the guest list blank.

You're invited to:

Date:
Friday, May 25

Time:
7:00 to midnight

Place:
The Butterfly Lounge
2501 4th Street

Cleo's Birthday Party

Come and celebrate my 22nd birthday at the Butterfly Lounge. The food, music, and drinks are free!

Guest List:

Kathy   Maria & Carlos
Yu Kim   Kenichi
Marithe   Yang & Jenny

Word Bank
have / *go to* a birthday / dinner / holiday party

B Put your invitation on the classroom wall. Read the other invitations.

• Which parties are interesting to you? Write your name on the guest list.

• Write information about your party choices on a piece of paper.

C  Tell a partner about your party choices. Why do you want to go to these parties?

> Let's go to Cleo's birthday party on Friday night. The Butterfly Lounge is fun, and the food and drinks are free.

> Great idea! Let's go together.

10 HOME

A stained glass house in Brooklyn, the United States

Look at the photo. Answer the questions.

1 What do you see?

2 Who lives here?

3 Do you like this house? Why or why not?

UNIT GOALS

1 Identify objects and rooms in a home

2 Show surprise

3 Describe rooms in a house

4 Talk about ways to improve a room or house

Many modern apartments have to use space in creative ways.

1 VIDEO Small Spaces, Small Ideas

A Look at the photo. Is the room big or small? Is it a comfortable room? Do you like it? Tell a partner.

B Watch the video with the sound off. You will see three rooms. Check the *two* things you see people doing in each room.

Room 1	Room 2	Room 3
☐ reading	☐ cooking	☐ studying
☐ playing	☐ watching TV	☐ watching TV
☐ cooking	☐ eating and drinking	☐ sleeping

C Watch the video again. Is each room comfortable or not?

D Explain your answers in **C** to a partner.

> I don't like room 2. It's very dark.

2 VOCABULARY

A 🔄 Look at the apartment. With a partner, use the list to identify the different rooms, areas, and items.

ROOMS	AREAS
1. living room	6. balcony
2. dining room	7. elevator
3. kitchen	8. stairs
4. bedroom	9. yard
5. bathroom	10. garage

ITEMS		
a. sofa	f. wall	k. refrigerator
b. rug	g. window	l. stove
c. lamp	h. air conditioner	m. toilet
d. table	i. closet	n. sink
e. chair	j. bed	o. shower

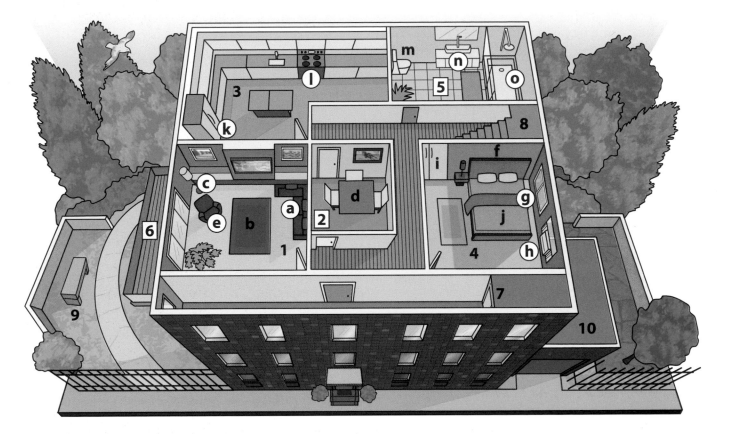

B 🔄 Cover up the lists in **A**. Can you and your partner identify the different rooms, areas, and items?

C 🔄 Ask and answer the questions with a partner.

1. What rooms are in your apartment or house?

2. Where are items *d*, *g*, and *i* in your home?

3. Where do you watch TV? cook? hang out with friends? sleep? eat dinner? take a shower?

> I usually hang out with my friends in the living room.

> My family cooks dinner in the kitchen.

3 LISTENING

A 🔊 🔁 **Pronunciation: Rising intonation to show surprise.** You can show surprise by repeating certain information with rising intonation (↗). Listen and repeat. Then practice the dialogs with a partner. **CD 2 Track 24**

1. A: The rent is 2,000 a month.
   B: Two thousand? ↗ That's expensive!
2. A: There's no elevator in the building.
   B: No elevator? ↗ But you live on the sixth floor!
3. A: I live on a houseboat.
   B: A houseboat? ↗ That's cool!

B Look at the pictures in **D**. Name the rooms in each apartment.

C 🔊 **Listen for gist.** Yao is a student in Vancouver, Canada. He needs a place to live. Listen and check (✓) the correct answers. **CD 2 Track 25**

CITY RENTALS

Name: Yao Peng Wong   **Job:** Student

I want to rent...	❑ a house.	❑ an apartment.	❑ a room in a house.
I want to rent for...	❑ a month.	❑ nine months.	❑ twelve months.
I want to live...	❑ alone.	❑ with a roommate.	❑ with a family member.

D 🔊 **Listen for details.** Amy is telling Yao about three apartments. Listen and notice the rooms as Amy talks. Number the apartments 1–3. **CD 2 Track 26**

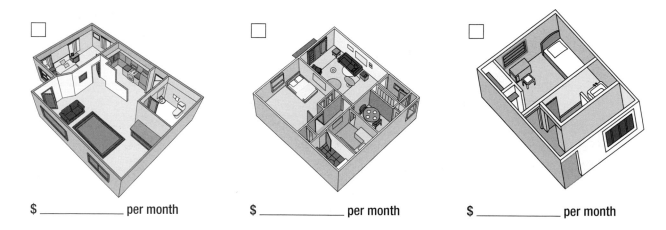

$ _____ per month $ _____ per month $ _____ per month

E 🔊 🔁 **Listen for numbers.** Listen again. Write the rent amount per month for each apartment in **D**. Circle the apartment Yao likes. What do you think of Yao's choice? Tell a partner. **CD 2 Track 26**

4 SPEAKING

A  **Listen for a speaker's attitude.** In the conversation, Tim uses two expressions (underlined) to show surprise. Listen. Notice how Tim says these expressions. **CD 2 Track 27**

TIM: Hey, Yao. How are you doing?

YAO: Hi, Tim. Come in.

TIM: Thanks. So, this is your new place. It's nice.

YAO: Yeah, and it's only $625 a month.

TIM: <u>Are you serious</u>? 625? That's cheap.

YAO: Yeah, *and* I've got free WiFi.

TIM: <u>No way</u>!

YAO: It's true. I've got a great apartment. There's just one problem.

TIM: What's that?

YAO: There's no elevator, and I'm on the sixth floor!

B Practice the conversation with a partner.

SPEAKING STRATEGY

C Make two new conversations with a partner. Use the Useful Expressions and the conversation above. Pay attention to your intonation (↗ or ↘).

Useful Expressions: Showing surprise	
Said with rising intonation ↗	Said with falling intonation ↘
My house has 20 rooms.	My house has 20 rooms.
Really?	You're kidding. / You're joking.
Are you serious?	No way. [informal]
For real? [informal]	(No,) it's true.
Yeah.	

Word Bank
I **live in** a house / an apartment building.
I **live on** the first / second / third / top floor.

D Read the examples below. Then tell four people something they don't know about you. If you cannot think of anything, make something up.

A: I play the guitar.

B: For real?

A: Yeah. I play in a band.

B: Where do you practice?

A: My sister lives near a famous soccer player.

B: You're kidding.

A: No, it's true.

B: What's his name?

E Which answer from **D** is the most interesting or unusual? Tell the class.

A Turn to page 212. Complete the exercises. Then do **B–D** below.

There is / There are				
Singular	**There is** (There's) / **There isn't**	a	rug	in my bedroom.
Plural	**There are** / **There aren't** any		rugs	

Questions	Short answers
Is there an elevator in your building?	Yes, **there is**. / No, **there isn't**.
Are there (any) windows in your living room?	Yes, **there are**. / No, **there aren't** (any).
How many windows **are (there)** in your bedroom?	**There's** one. / **There are** two. / **There aren't** any.

B Work with a partner. Look at the chart below. On a piece of paper, make as many sentences as you can.

There	are / aren't / is / isn't	a / any / some / two	chairs / sofa / TV / windows	in the living room.

> How many rooms are in your house?
>
> There are ten.
>
> Is there a bedroom?
>
> There are three bedrooms.

C Imagine your dream house. Answer the questions.

- How many rooms are there in your house? What are the rooms?

- What items are in each room?

D Take turns asking and answering questions with a partner. Talk about your dream house.

Adare Manor, Limerick, Ireland

6 COMMUNICATION

A Look at the picture and read about the bedroom.

In my room, the bed is **near** a big window. The window is **to the right** of the bed. Next to the bed (**on the right**), there's a small table with a lamp **on** it. There is also a table **to the left** of the bed. There is a mirror **above** my bed and a chair **in front of** my bed.

B 🔁 Talk about your room with a partner.

Student A: Think about your bedroom. On a piece of paper, draw your bedroom door and your bed. Then give the paper to your partner. What other things are in your room? Where are they? Tell your partner.

Student B: Listen to your partner's description. Draw your partner's bedroom.

C 🔁 **Student A:** Check your partner's drawing. Does it look like your room? Switch roles and do **B** again. Are your rooms similar or different?

Word Bank
mirror = a flat piece of glass that reflects things

1 VOCABULARY

A  Say the colors with your instructor. Then ask a partner: What is your favorite color?

B Look at the photo. Answer the questions with a partner.

1. What things are in the room? What colors are they?

2. When you look at the room, how do you feel?
   Complete this sentence with a word from the box.
   This room makes me feel _____.

3. Do you like the room? Why or why not?

> The colors are very bright. They make me feel happy. I like the room.

Word Bank
Opposites (feelings)
relaxed ↔ nervous, uncomfortable
happy ↔ unhappy, sad

C Find another photo of a room in a house. Answer the questions in **B** about it with a partner.

2 LISTENING

A 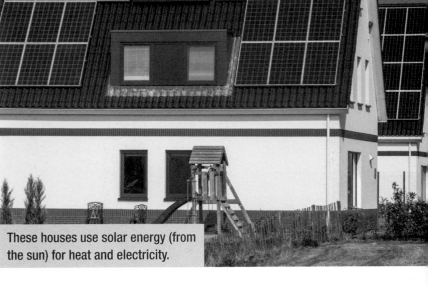 Look up the word *energy* in your dictionary. Then ask a partner: Does your home use a lot of energy?

These houses use solar energy (from the sun) for heat and electricity.

B 🔊 **Make and check predictions.** You will hear a man talk about a "green home." Read the sentence below and guess the answer(s). Then listen and circle the correct answer(s). **CD 2 Track 28**

A "green home" _____.

    a. saves energy

    b. is the color green

    c. is expensive

    d. is good for the environment (plants, land, water)

C 🔁 **Make predictions.** You want your house to be more "green." How can you do it? Look at the photos and read the sentences. Guess the answers with a partner.

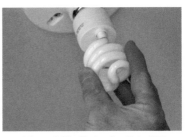

Word Bank
Word partnerships
If you *save energy*, you use less energy.
You can also *save money* and *water*.

1. Unplug your _____, _____, and _____.

2. Use CFL light bulbs. They use _____ energy.

3. When you leave a room, always turn _____ the lights.

4. Take _____-minute showers.

D 🔊 **Listen for details.** Listen to the full interview. Complete the sentences in **C**. **CD 2 Track 29**

E 🔁 Do you do any of the things in **C** in your house? Tell a partner.

3 READING

A 🔄 **Make predictions.** Read the title of the article and the question below it. Guess the answers below with a partner. One set of colors is extra.

Room	A good color for the room
1. bedroom	a. red, orange, or yellow
2. living room	
3. dining room	b. white only
4. kitchen	c. light blue, light green, or light purple
5. home office / study room	
	d. white and light blue

B **Check predictions.** Read the passage. Check your answers in **A**.

C **Scan for information.** Complete the chart with the correct colors and feelings.

Room color(s)	Feeling(s)
light blue, light green, or light purple	1. _____
2. _____ _____	alert, sometimes 3. _____, and happy
lots of dark or bright colors	4. _____
5. _____ walls and _____ lights	uncomfortable
6. light _____ and _____	relaxed and ready to study

D 🔄 Answer the questions with a partner. Use ideas from the reading.

1. Look at the photo. Is this room good for studying? relaxing? eating? Why?

2. Answer the questions above about a room in your house.

We see color everywhere. It makes our world beautiful, but it can also affect[1] our feelings and behavior.[2] For this reason, it is important to use the right colors in different rooms in a home. For example, light colors—like light blue, green, or purple—relax us. They are perfect in a bedroom or living room.

Other colors—like red, orange, and yellow—are different. They make us feel alert[3] and sometimes hungry, studies show. For this reason, they can be good to use in a dining area or a kitchen.

A room with some red, orange, or yellow can also feel happy and can be good in a living area. But these colors are very strong,[4] and it's best to only use a little of them. People feel nervous in rooms with too many dark or bright colors.

Other colors help us work or study. Many people think white walls and bright lights are best for this. But people are often uncomfortable in this kind of room. It is hard to sit and think. Instead, use white with another color, especially light blue. This color relaxes people. In a home office or a room for studying, light blue and white can help people think better.

[1] If something *affects* you, it changes you in some way.
[2] Your *behavior* is the way you act.
[3] If you are *alert*, you feel very awake and ready to do things.
[4] A *strong* color is bright or intense.

4 GRAMMAR

A Turn to page 213. Complete the exercises. Then do **B** and **C** below.

			very / too			
	Verb	**a / an**	**very / too**	**Adjective / Adverb**	**Noun**	**to + Verb**
This room	is		**very / too**	dark.		
He	talks		**too**	fast. I don't understand.		
I	am		**too**	tired		to watch TV.
They	have	a	**very**	big	house.	

B 🔄 Write two sentences about each photo with a partner. Use *too* or *very*. Put your sentences on the board.

C 🔄 Read the sentences on the board. Do you agree with them? Are any incorrect? If yes, correct them with a partner.

This is a very colorful room.

Yeah, but the colors are too bright.

5 WRITING

A Read about an apartment in Santiago. Then write about your house or apartment.

> I live with my family in an apartment in Santiago. We live on the 6th floor. There are two bedrooms in the apartment. I share one with my sister. In our room, there are two beds, a desk, a bookshelf, and a closet. It's too small for all our clothes! The apartment also has a living room, dining area, a kitchen, and a very big balcony with lots of plants. I like our apartment a lot!

B 🔄 Share your writing with a partner. Correct any mistakes in his or her writing.

C 🔄 Return your partner's paper. Then explain: Are your homes similar or different? Give examples.

6 COMMUNICATION

A The TV show *Room Redo* helps a person change a room in his or her home to make it better. Look at the room. Read about this week's person.

B 🔄 Work with a partner. You work for *Room Redo*. What are the problems with Felix's dorm room? How can you fix these problems? On a piece of paper, list and then draw your ideas.

> The walls are too.... Let's....

C 👥 Work with another pair. Explain your ideas to them. When you listen, take notes. What do you like about their ideas?

D 👥 Repeat **C** with three other pairs. At the end, review your notes. Then ask a partner: Whose room redo is the best? Why?

Name: Felix Hernandez (male)
Age: 22
Job: Student
His room: Felix lives in a dorm room at City University.

11 CLOTHING

A group of fashion models wearing colorful outfits

Look at the photo. Answer the questions.

1 What colors are the clothes?

2 Where are these people?

3 Would you wear clothes like these?

UNIT GOALS

1 Identify clothing and accessories

2 Ask for and give prices of things

3 Describe clothing and personal style

4 Talk about dress codes

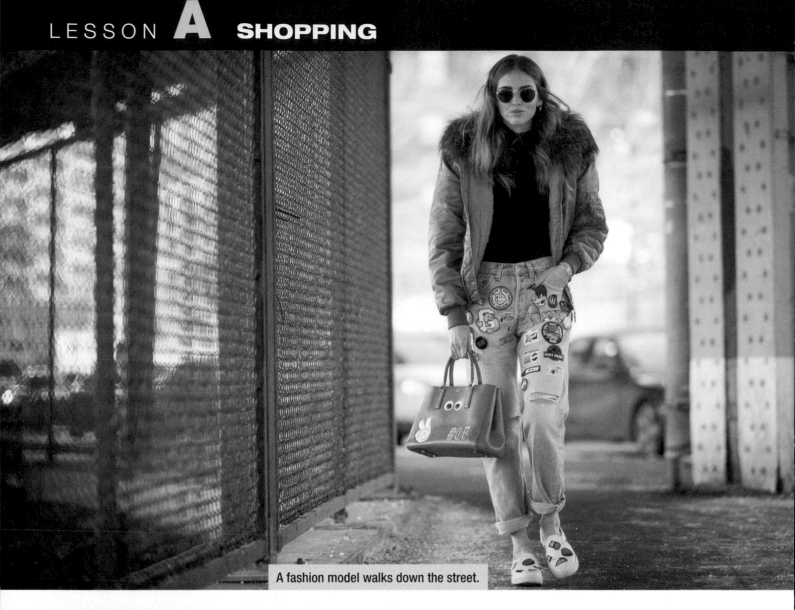

A fashion model walks down the street.

1 VIDEO Street Style in New York City

A ▶ 🔄 Watch the video. Then answer the questions with a partner.

1. Where are the people?
2. Do you like their clothes? Why or why not?
3. Do people in your city dress like the people in the video?

B ▶ 🔄 Watch the video again. What pieces of clothing do you see in the video? Do you know any of the words in English? Make a list with a partner.

C 👥 Share your ideas in **B** with the class.

2 VOCABULARY

A  Say the words in the box with your instructor. Tell a partner what each person is wearing. Then talk about what you are wearing.

> He's wearing a T-shirt, jeans, and a pair of sandals.

a. T-shirt
b. jeans*
c. sandals*
d. dress
e. heels*
f. jacket
g. pants*
h. sneakers*
i. shorts*
j. socks*
k. boots*
l. blouse
m. skirt
n. shirt
o. suit
p. coat
q. belt
r. hat
s. sweater / pullover
t. scarf
u. gloves*
v. uniform

*a pair of (item)

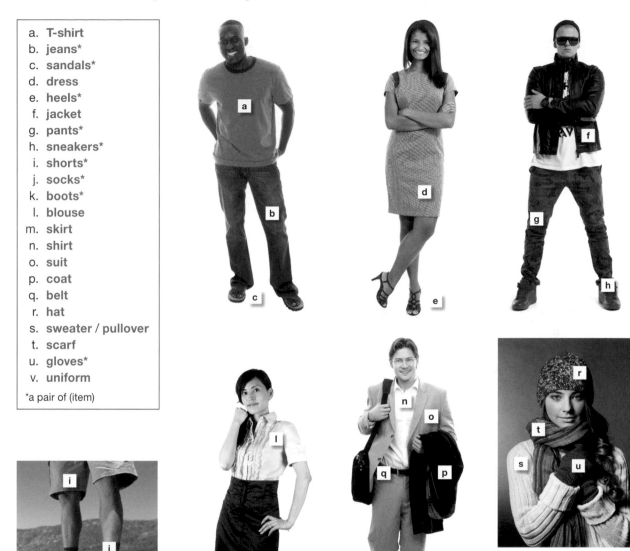

B  Cover up the list of words. Look at the pictures again. How many kinds of shoes can you name? How many pieces of clothing? How many accessories? Make lists with a partner.

Word Bank
Word partnerships
a pair of sunglasses / headphones / chopsticks

Word Bank
accessory = item worn or carried that is not clothing, for example, jewelry or a hat

3 LISTENING

A 🗣 With a partner, name the clothes in the store windows below. Are any of the clothes your style?

Word Bank

If certain clothes *are your style*, you like to wear them.

Word Bank

window-shopping = to look at items in a store window

B 🔊 **Listen for gist.** Listen to Rafa and Lucy as they go window-shopping. **CD 2 Track 31**

1. Write *1, 2,* or *3* in the correct window. One picture is extra.

2. Circle the store Rafa and Lucy go in.

C 🔊 **Listen for details.** Listen again. Circle the best answer to complete each sentence.
CD 2 Track 31

1. Lucy likes / doesn't like the T-shirt.

2. She likes / doesn't like the sandals.

3. She likes / doesn't like the blouse.

4. She is / isn't looking for summer clothes.

5. It is / isn't her brother's birthday soon.

6. She likes / doesn't like the boots.

D 🗣 Answer the questions with a partner.

• What is a good area for window-shopping in your city?

• What are the best stores?

• What can you buy there?

4 SPEAKING

A 🔊 Jin is from South Korea. He's in Rome now on vacation. Listen. Then answer the questions. **CD 2 Track 32**

1. What is Jin doing?

2. What doesn't Jin want? How does he say that? Underline the words.

3. What does Jin buy? How does he say it? Circle the words.

STORE CLERK: *Buon giorno.*

JIN: Um, hello. Do you speak English?

STORE CLERK: Yes, I do. Can I help you?

JIN: Oh, yeah... thanks. I'm shopping for a gift for my sister. I want to get something Italian.

STORE CLERK: I see. Well, we have some nice traditional scarves.

JIN: Yeah, they are nice. How much are they?

STORE CLERK: Sixty euros.

JIN: Sixty euros? Um... I'll think about it.

STORE CLERK: We also have T-shirts... like this Roma one.

JIN: Oh, that's cool. How much is it?

STORE CLERK: Nineteen euros.

JIN: That's perfect. I'll take it.

B 🔄 Practice the conversation with a partner.

SPEAKING STRATEGY

C 🔄 Imagine you're on vacation in Italy. You want to buy a gift for someone. With a partner, make a new conversation.

- **Shopper:** Who are you shopping for? Tell the clerk.

- **Store clerk:** Show the shopper at least three items. Use the prices below. Try to make a sale!
  €300   €40   €35   €95   €235

D 🔄 Switch roles and do **C** again.

Trajan's Forum, Rome, Italy

Useful Expressions
Saying what you want
I'm looking for a gift for my sister.
Asking for and giving prices
How much are they?
They're 60 euros.
Thanks, I'll think about it.
How much is the T-shirt?
It's 19 euros.
I'll take it.
Speaking Tip
When you're not looking for anything in particular:
Can I help you?
No thanks, I'm just looking.

5 GRAMMAR

A Turn to page 214. Complete the exercises. Then do **B–E** below.

want to / have to	
1. I **want** <u>these boots</u>. They're cool.	*want* + noun
2. I **want to** <u>buy</u> these boots. They're cool.	*want to* + verb
3. I **have** <u>a coat</u>. It's in the closet.	*have* + noun
4. I **have to** <u>buy</u> a coat. I don't have one.	*have to* + verb

B Read the sentences in the chart above. Then circle *yes* or *no* about each of the statements below.

- Sentences 1 and 2 have the same meaning.   yes   no

- Sentences 3 and 4 have the same meaning.   yes   no

- Sentence 4 means something is necessary.   yes   no

> **i** In spoken English, *want to* can sound like "wanna." *Have to* can sound like "hafta."

C 🔊 ⟳ **Pronunciation: *Want to* and *have to*.** Work with a partner. Listen and repeat. Then complete the sentences with *want to* or *have to*. **CD 2 Track 33**

1. I _____ buy a new belt. This one is old.

2. I _____ visit Jamaica or Puerto Rico this summer.

3. It's a formal party. You _____ wear a jacket and tie.

4. I have free time now. Do you _____ do something?

D You are going to go skiing in Switzerland. Look at your checklist. What things do you already have? Check them off.

E ⟳ Take turns telling a partner about your list. What are two things that are not necessary that you want to take anyway?

> *My Travel Checklist*
> - a hat and gloves
> - jeans
> - a passport
> - a place to stay
> - a plane ticket
> - skis
> - sneakers
> - sunglasses
> - sweaters
> - Swiss money
> - a warm jacket and boots

> I don't have a passport.
> I have to get one.

> I want to get a new
> pair of skis.

6 COMMUNICATION

A Read the questions and think about your answers.

1. Do you buy clothes often? Where do you shop? How much do you usually spend?

2. Complete this sentence: If you want to speak English well, you have to _____.

3. Look at three people in your class. What are they wearing?

4. What is something you want to do this year?

5. At school or work, do you have to wear a uniform? Are there things you cannot wear?

6. Think about the clothes in your closet. Which clothing item is your favorite? Why?

7. Is it OK for men to wear jewelry (rings, earrings)? What jewelry looks good on a man? What jewelry only looks good on a woman? Why?

B 🔅 Work with three or four other people.

1. Take turns. Choose a question from **A**.

2. Answer the question. If you can talk for one minute without stopping, you get one point.

3. Continue until there are no more questions. The winner is the person with the most points.

Word Bank
jewelry = decoration worn on the body
earrings = jewelry worn on the ears
ring = jewelry worn on the fingers

Even at school, I usually wear something kind of **dressy**.

What's your personal **style**?

I like **casual** clothes— something I can **put on** quickly in the morning.

1 VOCABULARY

A 🔄 What are the people wearing? With a partner, match the items below with the photos.

a **light** shirt with **short** sleeves

baggy sweatpants

fitted jeans

B 🔄 Answer the questions with a partner.

1. Describe your classmates' clothes. Use words in the box.

2. What's your personal style—dressy or casual? What do you usually wear?

3. After work or school, do you change your clothes? What do you put on?

> I put on baggy shorts and a fitted shirt with long sleeves.

Word Bank
Opposites
baggy / loose ↔ **fitted / tight**
casual ↔ **dressy / formal**
heavy ↔ **light**
long ↔ **short**
put on ↔ **take off**

Word Bank
put on = to place clothes or shoes on your body to wear
change clothes = to take off your clothes and put on different clothes

2 LISTENING

A 🔁 Read the definitions. Then answer the questions with a partner.

> If you *change (your) clothes,* you take off your clothes and put on different clothes.
>
> If your clothes *match,* they look good together.

1. Do you change your clothes during the day?
2. Do the clothes you're wearing today match?

a tie

a job interview

B 🔁 **Make predictions.** Look at the pictures. With a partner, answer the questions.

1. What is the man wearing in each of the pictures below?
2. Which clothes are best for a job interview? Why?

C 🔊 **Listen for gist.** Diego has a job interview. Listen. At the beginning, what clothes is he wearing? Write *1* next to the picture above. At the end, what is he wearing? Write *2* next to the picture. One picture is extra. **CD 2 Track 34**

D 🔊 **Listen for details.** Diego changes his clothes. Why? Listen again and match the clothes (1–4) with the reasons (a–d). **CD 2 Track 34**

1. jacket _____   a. too formal
2. pants _____   b. doesn't match
3. tie _____   c. has coffee on it
4. shirt _____   d. too dark

E 🔁 **Infer information.** What clothing is best for a woman to wear to an interview? Tell a partner.

3 READING

A 🔄 **Make predictions.** Read *only* Tomas's post on the next page. Then answer the questions with a partner.

1. Where is Tomas from? Where does he want to go?

2. Guess the answer to Tomas's question. Make a list of ideas.

B 🔄 **Read for details.** Read Rayyan's reply. Which items (1–6) are good for Tomas to pack? Circle them. Which aren't? Put an *X*. Explain your answers to a partner.

1. T-shirts

2. a short skirt

3. long, baggy pants

4. an umbrella

5. a shirt with long sleeves

6. shoes you can take off easily

C 🔄 **Infer meaning.** Find the underlined words in the reading. Complete the "a" sentences with the correct word. Then answer the "b" questions with a partner.

1a. If you wear <u>suitable</u> clothes, they are / aren't right for a situation.

1b. What clothes are suitable for school? Which aren't?

2a. A shirt with short / long sleeves <u>covers</u> your arms.

2b. What other clothing can cover your arms?

3a. An umbrella / A bathing suit <u>protects</u> you from the sun.

3b. What else can protect you from the sun?

4a. If something <u>fits</u>, it is comfortable / uncomfortable to wear.

4b. What makes a piece of clothing fit well?

WHAT
DO I PACK?

Tomas	Δ Posted: Saturday May 17
Location:	**What do I pack[1]?**
Chile	I plan to visit Malaysia in June (when it's 30–33 degrees Celsius). I know many people in Malaysia are Muslim, and I need information about clothing customs.[2] Is it OK to wear shorts and T-shirts in most places? What about for women?

Δ Posted: Saturday May 17

Rayyan Tomas — Here's some advice:

Location:
Malaysia

- It's hot here, especially in the summer, so light clothing is best. At the beach and other touristy areas, the style is casual. Many people wear shorts and T-shirts there. Also, it rains in some places in early June, sometimes a lot. Bring an umbrella and maybe a light jacket. A hat is also good.

- In Kuala Lumpur and other cities, casual clothes are okay, but they should **cover** you. For women, it's best not to wear short dresses or skirts in public. Long, loose pants (or a long skirt for women) and light shirts or blouses are often best. They're more **suitable**. These clothes also **protect** you from the sun!

- Bring a pair of comfortable shoes and some sandals, or buy some here. (Be sure to try on shoes first to make sure they **fit**; sizes can be different from your country.) And remember: you have to take off your shoes in some buildings, like temples and people's houses.

- Do you plan to attend a formal event? If yes, bring a nice pair of pants, a shirt with long sleeves, and a tie. For women, a long dress is best.

Hope this helps!

[1] If you *pack* clothes for travel, you put them in a suitcase or bag to take with you.

[2] A *custom* is a common, traditional activity in a certain country or place.

People with traditional Malaysian clothing and kites

4 GRAMMAR

A Turn to page 215. Complete the exercises. Then do **B** and **C** below.

Count Nouns	Noncount Nouns
This **shirt is** / These **shirts are** expensive.	This **clothing is** expensive.
This ring is **a dollar** / **two dollars**.	I want to save **money**. (Not: ~~a money~~)
I need (**some**) new winter **boots**.	I need (**some**) **luggage** for my trip.
I have **a pair of sunglasses**. He has **ten pairs of shoes** in his closet.	**a piece of** / **two pieces of jewelry**

B Carmen's parents want to give her a gift. Look at the things Carmen wants. Next to each item, write *a, some, a pair of, a piece of,* or nothing. Sometimes, more than one answer is possible.

Carmen wants…

1. _____ new scarf.
2. _____ money.
3. _____ new clothes.
4. _____ new sneakers.
5. _____ furniture for her bedroom.
6. _____ bag.
7. _____ jewelry.
8. _____ sunglasses.

C 👥 Work in a small group.

- One person begins. Suggest something to give Carmen from **B**. Explain your answer.
- If you make a correct sentence, you get a point.
- If the sentence is incorrect, another person can correct it and get a point.
- Then the next person takes a turn.
- Talk about all the items. The winner is the person with the most points.

> Let's give her some money. Money is good for a college student.

> Or we can get her a new clothes.

> Wait, "a new clothes" isn't correct. We can get her *some* new clothes. Let's buy a scarf.

5 WRITING

A On a piece of paper, write about the things you are wearing.

Describe...

- your clothes and their colors and style.
- other things you are wearing—jewelry, glasses, a hat, etc.

> I'm wearing a pair of fitted jeans, a gray T-shirt, a heavy sweater, and a hat. My socks are white and my boots are black. I'm also wearing some jewelry.

B Give your paper to your instructor. Your instructor gives you another student's paper. Read it. Correct any mistakes. Then guess the writer. Give the paper to that person.

6 COMMUNICATION

A Read about these two items. Which is interesting to you? Tell a partner.

How much exercise are you getting? This wristband shows you. Most people put on the fitness band and never take it off!

This clothing changes color and shows others your feelings. When you're happy or relaxed, it's blue. When you're nervous, it's red.

B With a partner, research an interesting type of clothing, jewelry, or accessory. Find a photo of it. Then answer these questions:

1. What kind of clothing, jewelry, or accessory is it?
2. Who is it for (men, women, children, everyone)?
3. What does it do?
4. How much does it cost?
5. Why do you like it?

C Present your idea to the class. Then listen to your classmates talk about their ideas. For each item, answer questions 1–5 in **B**. Which one is your favorite?

12 JOBS

Look at the photo. Answer the questions.

1 What is the man's job?

2 Is this job hard or easy?

3 Do you want to do a job like this? Why or why not?

UNIT GOALS

1 Identify and describe jobs

2 Talk about where you work and who you work for

3 Describe your work goals

4 Talk about things you can and can't do

A blacksmith demonstrates his metal work, Memphis, the United States.

A stunt pilot doing a trick. Would you want to do this job?

1 VIDEO Career Day

A Look at the jobs below. Which do you know? Look up the ones you don't know in a dictionary.

☐ a doctor   ☐ a surfer   ☐ a veterinarian   ☐ the president

☐ an actress   ☐ a pilot   ☐ a lawyer   ☐ a musician

☐ a web designer   ☐ a photographer   ☐ a filmmaker   ☐ a baseball player

B ▶ Watch the video with the sound off. Guess: What jobs do the students want to do? Check (✓) your answers in **A**.

C ▶ Watch the video with the sound on. Check your answers in **B**.

D 🔁 Choose the job you want to do in **A**. Tell a partner.

> I want to be a pilot. It's an exciting job.

2 VOCABULARY

A 🔁 Look at the pictures below. Then follow these instructions:

- Cover the chart and look at the pictures. Can you name any of the jobs?

- Check your answers. Practice saying the jobs with a partner.

> He's a doctor.

Nouns ending in *-er* / *-or* or *-ist* often describe a job or something a person does.		
-er / -or	1. **doctor** 4. **telemarketer**	2. **web designer** 5. **police officer**	3. **programmer** 6. **lawyer**
-ist	7. **receptionist**	8. **hairstylist**	
person	9. **businessperson**	10. **delivery person**	
other	11. **flight attendant**	12. **nurse**	

B 🔁 Look at the jobs in **A**. Answer the questions with a partner.

1. Which jobs make the most money?

2. Which jobs are easy? Which ones are hard?

3. Do you know anyone with these jobs?

3 LISTENING

A 🔄 In your country, do students ever go to school *and* work? Discuss with a partner.

B 🔊 **Listen for details.** Yana is a student. She is looking for a job. Read the question below. Then listen and circle the correct answer. **CD 2 Track 36**

When can Yana work?

    a. on some weekdays and all weekend

    b. on some weekdays but not on the weekend

    c. only on Saturdays and Sundays

C 🔊 **Listen for details.** Listen and complete the information about each job. **CD 2 Track 37**

Jobs		
Job 1: a waitress at the Sunflower _____ Days/hours: from _____ to _____ in the _____	Job 2: a tutor at the _____ Days/hours: _____ or _____	Job 3: a cashier in a _____ store Days/hours: on _____ from _____ to _____

Word Bank
Word partnerships with *job*   **look for / get / have / find** a job   a **part-time** / a **full-time** job

D 🔄 **Draw conclusions.** Look at your answers in **B** and **C**. Which jobs are good for Yana? Why? Tell a partner.

E 🔄 Read this list of different places to work. Where do you want to work? Rate the places from 1 (like a lot) to 6 (don't like very much). Tell a partner.

    _____ in a cafe

    _____ at school

    _____ in a clothing store

    _____ at home

    _____ in an office

    _____ outdoors

Word Bank
cashier = the person who gives and receives money at a store   *tutor* = a teacher for one student   *waiter / waitress* = someone who brings food and takes orders at a restaurant

4 SPEAKING

A 🔊 Valentina and Brad are at Ramon's party. Listen to their conversation. Then answer the questions. **CD 2 Track 38**

1. What does Valentina do? (What's her job?)

2. Does she like her job? Why or why not?

VALENTINA: Hi, are you a friend of Ramon's?

BRAD: Yeah, hi. My name is Brad.

VALENTINA: Hi, Brad. I'm Valentina.

BRAD: Valentina... I know you.... You're Ramon's friend, too, right? You're a chef at that restaurant, The Boulevard....

VALENTINA: Yeah, that's me. But I'm not a chef anymore.

BRAD: Really? What do you do now?

VALENTINA: I work for a company called The Olive Kitchen. It imports food from Italy, Greece, and Turkey.

BRAD: Wow, what's that like?

VALENTINA: It's great. I travel, meet interesting people, and eat good food!

B 🔄 Practice the conversation with a partner.

C 🔊 🔄 **Pronunciation: Reduced words.** Work with a partner. Practice saying these two questions. Then listen and repeat. **CD 2 Track 39**

What do you do?   Where do you work?

D 🔊 🔄 **Pronunciation: Reduced words.** Listen and fill in the missing words. Then practice the dialogs with a partner. **CD 2 Track 40**

A: What do you do?

B: I'm a _____.

A: Where do you work?

B: In a _____ downtown.

A: What do you do?

B: I'm a _____.

A: Where do you work?

B: In a large _____.

> ℹ️ In spoken English, small words like *do* and *you* are often reduced. Reduced forms are short. They sound different.

> ℹ️ In questions, *do* is reduced from /du/ to /də/

SPEAKING STRATEGY

E 🔄 Use the Useful Expressions to complete the dialogs below. Then read the dialogs with a partner.

1. A: So, what _____ do?

   B: I _____ Apple. _____ a programmer.

2. A: What _____ your parents _____?

   B: My mom works _____ a bank. My dad works _____ Samsung.

Useful Expressions
Talking about jobs
What do you / does she do?
I'm a student. / She's a nurse.
I work for myself. / She works for Telefonica.
I work in / She works in a hospital / an office / a cafe.

F 🔄 Create a new dialog with a partner. Use a job that you'd like to do. Then change roles and repeat.

5 GRAMMAR

A Turn to page 216. Complete the exercise. Then do **B–D** below.

Questions with *like*	
1. A: My mom works in a hospital.	2. A: My coworker is from Brazil.
B: Really? **What's** that **like**?	B: Oh? **What's** he **like**?
A: It's hard, but she enjoys it.	A: He's really nice.

B Read the two dialogs in the chart above. Pay attention to the questions. Which question asks about an experience? Which question asks about a person?

C 🔄 What are the jobs below like? Take turns talking about each job with a partner. Use the words in the chart to help you.

1. police officer
2. pilot
3. flight attendant

4. telemarketer
5. delivery person
6. your idea: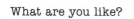

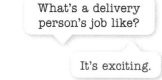

> What's a delivery person's job like?

> It's exciting.

Words to describe experiences	Words to describe people	
fun / exciting / cool / interesting ↔ boring	friendly / nice ↔ unfriendly	cool / interesting ↔ boring
safe ↔ dangerous	fun ↔ serious	shy ↔ outgoing
easy ↔ hard	hardworking ↔ lazy	strict ↔ easygoing

D 🔄 What are these people like? Take turns talking about the people with a partner. Use the words from the chart in **C** to help you.

1. you
2. your classmates or coworkers
3. your parents

> What are you like?

> I think I'm a friendly person....

Some delivery people in cities use bikes to get around. It's a dangerous job!

6 COMMUNICATION

A 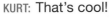 Practice the conversation with a partner. Then answer the questions about Elena. What does she do? Who does she work for? What's her job like?

KURT: So, what do you do, Elena?

ELENA: I'm a reporter. I work for a music show called *Que Colores*. Here's my card.

KURT: Oh, thanks. So, what's your job like?

ELENA: It's fun. I meet different artists and go to concerts and film festivals.

KURT: That's cool!

Word Bank
reporter = someone who gets stories for the news

B Think of your dream job. Make three identical business cards on three pieces of paper. Then answer the questions below about your job. Use the model above.

	Me	Partner 1	Partner 2	Partner 3
What do you do?				
Who do you work for?				
What's your job like?				

C Imagine you are at a party. Introduce yourself to three people. Give each person your business card. Then complete the chart in **B** with information about each person you meet.

D Which person has the most interesting job? Tell the class.

This summer, I'm **doing an internship** at a fashion-design company. I work **part-time** (ten hours a week). I don't **make** any money, but I'm **getting a lot of experience**. In the future, maybe I can **get a full-time job** with this company. That's my **goal**.

1 VOCABULARY

A 🔁 Read about Philippe's work goals. Tell a partner which things are true. Philippe...

1. works 40 hours a week.
2. works for free.
3. is learning to do a job.
4. has two jobs.
5. wants to work at the same place in the future.
6. wants to make money in the future.

> **Word Bank**
>
> *goal* = something you want to do in the future

> Philippe doesn't work 40 hours a week. He works part-time.

B Complete the sentences with your ideas.

My work goals (in the future)	
1. I want to get... ☐ a full-time job. ☐ a part-time job. ☐ a different job. ☐ some work experience.	2. I want to work in / for _____. I want to do an internship at _____. 3. Pay: I want to make _____ a year / an hour.

C 🔁 Tell a partner your answers in **B**. Are your goals the same?

> I want to get a part-time job this summer.

> In the future, I want to make $60,000 a year.

2 LISTENING

A 🔁 **Make predictions.** Look up the words in the box. Then look at two students' summer jobs below. Answer the questions with a partner.

1. Where do Yuko and Davi work? What do they do?

2. Guess: What are their job responsibilities and requirements?

coach	tour guide
requirement	volunteer
responsibility	

Name: Yuko Abe   **Age:** 21   **From:** Japan
Tour guide, Tokyo Disneyland

Job responsibilities:
- _____ people to the park
- Answer _____ about where to go

Job requirements:
- Speak _____ and basic _____

Pay: _____ yen per month

Name: Davi Santos   **Age:** 22   **From:** Brazil
Soccer coach, Madagascar

Job responsibilities:
- Teach _____ to play soccer

Job requirements:
- Be able to play _____
- Speak some _____ or _____

Pay: _____

B 🔊 **Listen for details.** Write a word or number in each blank in **A**. **CD 2 Track 41**

C 🔊 **Listen for a speaker's attitude.** Listen again. Circle the correct word in the first column. Then complete each word in the second. **CD 2 Track 41**

Word Bank
Large numbers
1,000   one thousand
10,000   ten thousand
100,000   one hundred thousand
1,000,000   one million

Do they like their jobs?	Why?
1. Yuko likes / doesn't like her job.	The job is f_____. She meets people from all over J_____ and the w_____
2. Davi likes / doesn't like his job.	The kids are g_____, the country is b_____, and he's l_____ a lot.

D 🔁 Are Yuko's and Davi's jobs interesting to you? Why or why not? Tell a partner.

> I like Yuko's job. You can get experience and make some money. And it's a fun place to work.

3 READING

A ⟳ **Make predictions.** Look at the title and photos on the next page. Guess: What does Michelle Phan do? Use ideas from the box.

> a. department store cashier
> b. waitress
> c. model
> d. businessperson
> e. makeup artist

B **Read for details.** Read the article. Then complete the sentences with the jobs (a–e) from **A**. Two answers are extra.

1. In college, Michelle Phan was a(n) _____.

2. Today, she's a(n) _____.

C ⟳ **Scan for information.** Ask and answer the questions with a partner. Find the answers quickly in the reading.

1. What do Michelle Phan's videos teach people?

2. How many people watch her videos?

3. Why is she popular?

4. How much money does she make a year?

5. In the future, what is her goal?

D ⟳ Answer the questions with a partner.

1. Name another entrepreneur. What does he or she do?

2. Do you have a hobby? Can you make money doing it? How?

INTERNET
ENTREPRENEUR
MICHELLE PHAN

An *entrepreneur* is a businessperson. Usually, he or she starts a new company.

Michelle Phan has one of the most popular channels on YouTube. Her videos teach people to put on makeup. A billion people have watched them.

Why is Phan so popular? She knows about makeup, of course. She also gives people helpful tips (what makeup to buy, how to look good with very little money, and many other ideas). But there's another reason: Phan is a regular[1] person, not a perfect model in a magazine. People watch her videos and they think, "I can look like her."

In addition to her YouTube channel, Phan now has her own makeup business (called "ipsy") and a line of makeup called "em." She also wrote a book and started a music business. In the future, she wants to start a new business, maybe in lifestyle or food.

YouTube entrepreneur Michelle Phan

Michelle Phan's work history:

- As a college student, she works as a waitress.

- She tries to get a job in a department store selling makeup, but she can't. She has no experience.

- In college, she starts making videos about makeup as a hobby.[2] Soon, thousands of people are watching them on YouTube.

- By age 27, she has a very popular channel and owns her own company. The company makes millions of dollars every year.

[1] A *regular* person is very similar to others.
[2] A *hobby* is something you do for fun.

Different types of makeup

A Turn to page 217. Complete the exercises. Then do **B–E** below.

Talking about Ability with *can / can't*		
Yes / No questions	**Can** you speak French?	Yes, I **can**. / No, I **can't**.
Wh- questions	Which languages **can** Carla speak?	(She **can** speak) Spanish and English.
	Who **can** speak Japanese?	Toshi (**can**).

B Read the job ad. Then complete the interview questions below. Write three *Yes / No* and two *Wh-* questions with *can*.

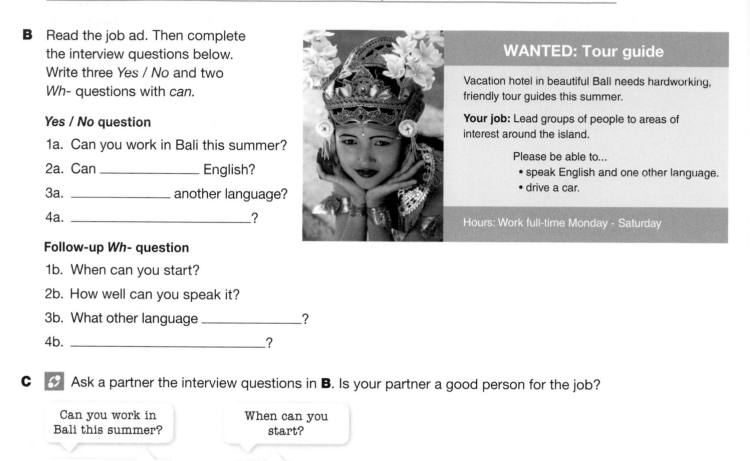

WANTED: Tour guide

Vacation hotel in beautiful Bali needs hardworking, friendly tour guides this summer.

Your job: Lead groups of people to areas of interest around the island.

Please be able to...
- speak English and one other language.
- drive a car.

Hours: Work full-time Monday - Saturday

Yes / No question

1a. Can you work in Bali this summer?

2a. Can _____ English?

3a. _____ another language?

4a. _____?

Follow-up Wh- question

1b. When can you start?

2b. How well can you speak it?

3b. What other language _____?

4b. _____?

C Ask a partner the interview questions in **B**. Is your partner a good person for the job?

> Can you work in Bali this summer?
>> Yes, I can.

> When can you start?
>> In June.

D Think of a job and make a new ad with your partner. Then write four or five interview questions with *can*.

E Get together with another pair.

1. Show them your job ad and questions. Read theirs.

2. Use your questions and interview one person from the other pair for your job. Your partner does the same. Take notes on the person's answers.

3. Compare notes with your partner. Which person is best for your job? Why?

5 WRITING

A Read the paragraph. Answer the questions with a partner.

1. What can he do well?

2. What are his goals? What does he want to be?

B Write about your work goals. Answer the questions in **A** about yourself. Exchange papers with a partner. Answer the questions in **A** about your partner. Correct any mistakes.

My work goals

I like comics and I can draw well. I usually draw my own characters. I practice every day. Right now, I'm majoring in digital art. In the future, I want to be a video game designer. Maybe I can do an internship first. Then I can get a full-time job and work for a big animation company. That's my goal.

6 COMMUNICATION

A Read the questions in the chart. Think about your answers.

Can you...

☐ speak and write well in your first language?
☐ remember phone numbers and names easily?
☐ tell interesting stories?

Group 1 Total: _____

☐ solve problems quickly?
☐ play chess well?
☐ do math quickly in your head?

Group 2 Total: _____

☐ play a musical instrument?
☐ read or write music?
☐ sing well?

Group 3 Total: _____

☐ fix or make things?
☐ draw or paint well?
☐ follow directions on a map?

Group 4 Total: _____

☐ exercise for 30 minutes a day?
☐ play a sport well?
☐ dance well?

Group 5 Total: _____

☐ give good advice?
☐ talk to new people easily?
☐ understand others' feelings?

Group 6 Total: _____

B Ask a partner the questions in the chart. Use *Can you....*
For your partner's answers, write a number:

3 = Yes, I can.   2 = Yes, a little.   1 = No, I can't.

> Can you play a musical instrument?

> Yes, I can.

C Now add the points for each group and write the totals.
Look at the chart below. What are good jobs for your partner?

7–9 points in...	Good jobs for you:
Group 1	teacher, lawyer, writer, salesperson, actor
Group 2	businessperson, programmer, doctor
Group 3	musician, DJ, singer

7–9 points in...	Good jobs for you:
Group 4	web designer, fashion designer, photographer, engineer
Group 5	dancer, athlete, coach
Group 6	teacher, manager, salesperson

D Look again at the chart in **A**. When did your partner say, "Yes, I can"? Ask your partner questions about these abilities.

> What instrument can you play?

> I can play the violin.

1 STORYBOARD

A Gary and Mina are at a party. Eun Mi and Carlos are shopping in Mexico City.
Complete the two conversations.

Conversation 1: Gary and Mina   **Conversation 2: Eun Mi and Carlos**

B 🔁 Practice the conversations with a partner.

C 🔁 Change roles and practice again.

2 SEE IT AND SAY IT

A 🔄 Study the picture. Take turns answering the questions with a partner.

1. What things are in the picture?
2. Look at the people in the picture. What are they wearing?

B 🔄 What are the people in the photo saying? Create a conversation with a partner.

> Excuse me. How much is that sofa?

> It's $2,000.

> Oh, that's too expensive!

3 SPOT THE DIFFERENCES

A  Look at the two pictures. What are the people doing? What are they wearing? What colors are the items? With a partner, find as many differences between the two pictures as you can in five minutes.

B How many did you see? Compare your ideas with another pair.

4 JOB ADS

A Look at the job ads. Can you do these jobs? Tell your partner.

> I can do the receptionist job.
> I can type quickly and...

Sundance Studio needs an outgoing dance teacher!

Teach children to dance

You: Friendly and outgoing dance teacher. Work well with children ages 6-8.

Days and hours: Thursday, Friday, and Saturday part-time, 5-9 PM.

Pay: $35 per hour

Wanted: Friendly, hardworking receptionist for an international office

You: Type quickly
Speak English on the phone
It helps if you can speak one of these languages: Chinese, Japanese, Korean, Portuguese, Russian, Spanish, or Thai.

Days and hours: Monday – Friday 8 AM – 5 PM.

Pay: $28,000 per year

B Now make your own job ad on a piece of paper. Write the name of the job, the responsibilities and requirements, the days and hours, and the pay.

C Put your ad on the classroom wall. Read the other ads. Which jobs can you do? Make a list.

D Tell a partner about the jobs on your list. Which jobs are good for you? Why?

5 WHAT DO YOU DO?

A 🔄 **Predict.** Look at the photos. Can you guess any information in the chart? Work with a partner.

Name	Job	Where	What's the job like?	Wants to...
Bill	_____	at a place called The Matrix	works _____	have his own _____ *restaurant*
Kira	works for herself	has a _____ store online	great, but she's _____ busy	get someone to _____ her
Juan	_____	in _____	sometimes _____	work during the _____
Diya	is doing an internship as a _____	at a tech company	interesting	get a _____ job there

B 🔊 **Listen for details.** Listen. Complete the chart above with the correct word(s). **CD 2 Track 43**

C 🔄 Answer the questions. Then ask a partner four *Wh-* questions of your own about the people.

1. What does Bill do?
2. Where does Juan work?
3. Who works for herself?
4. What is Juan's job like?
5. Who works a lot?
6. In the future, what does Diya want to do?

D 🔄 Work with a partner. Make a dialog between two people in the photos. Use the notes in the chart and your own ideas. Try to talk for two minutes.

> So, what do you do, Bill?

> I'm a chef.

> What's that like?

> It's interesting, but I have to work a lot.

LANGUAGE SUMMARIES

UNIT 1 INTRODUCTIONS

LESSON A

Vocabulary

classmate
email address
female / male
first name / last name
letters of the alphabet: A B C D E
  F G H I J K L M N O P Q R S T U
  V W X Y Z
Mr. / Ms. (Mrs. / Miss)
nickname
numbers 0–10: zero, one, two, three,
  four, five, six, seven, eight, nine, ten
phone number
student ID number
teacher

Speaking Strategy

Introducing yourself
Hi, what's your name?
  Hi, my name is Liling.
  I'm Liling. / It's Liling.
  I'm Alberto, but please call
  me Beto.
(It's) nice to meet you.
  (It's) nice to meet you, too.

How do you spell that /
your (last) name?
  It's (spelled) P-O-R-T-E-R.
What's your name?
  I'm Liling. / It's Liling.

LESSON B

Vocabulary

actor / actress
artist
author / writer
favorite (TV show)
**friend / be friends with
  (someone)**
movie
**music (classical, pop, rap,
  rock)**
(soccer) player
singer
**sport (baseball, basketball,
  soccer, tennis)**
team

UNIT 2 COUNTRIES

LESSON A

Vocabulary

(capital) city
country
nationality
(on) vacation

Argentina → Argentinean
Australia → Australian
Brazil → Brazilian
Canada → Canadian
Colombia → Colombian
Chile → Chilean
China → Chinese
Egypt → Egyptian
France → French
Japan → Japanese
Korea → Korean
Mexico → Mexican
New Zealand → New Zealander,
  Kiwi
Peru → Peruvian

Portugal → Portuguese
Spain → Spanish
Thailand → Thai
Turkey → Turkish
**the United Kingdom (the UK)
  → British**
**the United States (the US) →
  American**
Vietnam → Vietnamese

Speaking Strategy

Asking where someone is from
Where are you from?
  (I'm from) Japan.
Really? Where exactly? Which city? /
  Where in Japan?
    (I'm from) Tokyo / a small town
    near Tokyo.
Are you from Colombia?
  Yes, I am.
  No, I'm from Peru.

LESSON B

Vocabulary

beautiful
big
boring
busy
crowded
exciting
famous
friendly
fun
interesting
large
new
old
popular
relaxing
small
tall
wonderful

LESSON A

Vocabulary

backpack
bus pass
camera
cell phone
credit card
gift card
headphones
(student) ID
key
laptop
notebook
sunglasses
wallet
(expensive) watch

Speaking Strategy

**Giving and replying
 to thanks**
Thank you very much.
  You're welcome.
Thank you.
  My pleasure.
Thanks a lot.
  Sure, no problem.
Thanks.
  You bet.

LESSON B

Vocabulary

cheap ↔ expensive / valuable
comfortable ↔ uncomfortable
hard ↔ easy
important ↔ unimportant
keep ↔ throw out
messy ↔ clean

excellent / great
good
OK / so-so
bad
terrible

LESSON A

Vocabulary

do (homework)
dorm
drink (soda)
eat (pizza)
exercise
go (to school)
have a great time
improve
listen (to music)
roommate
shop
study (for a test)
talk (on the phone)
term
text (a friend)
watch TV

Speaking Strategy

**Greeting people and asking
  how they are**
Positive response
A: Hi, (Sara). How are you doing?
B: Fine. / OK. / All right. /
   Not bad. How about you?
A: I'm fine, thanks.

Negative response
A: Hi, (Yuki). How's it going?
B: So-so. / Not so good.
A: Really? / Yeah? What's
   wrong?
B: I'm waiting for the bus.
   It's late!

LESSON B

Vocabulary

**School subjects and college
  majors***
art
business
engineering
graphic design
history
information technology (IT)
law
math
nursing
science
tourism / hospitality

*A *school subject* is an area of study.
 Your *major* is your main subject of
 study in college.

Talking about your studies
Where do you go to school?
I go to / I'm a student at the
  Fashion Institute of Technology.

What are you studying?
I'm studying music / medicine.
I'm majoring in business.
I'm preparing for the college
  entrance exam.

What classes are you taking?
I'm taking a test-prep **class**. /
I'm taking two business
  classes.

LESSON A

Vocabulary

beans
bread
cheese
coffee
(fried) chicken
eggs
fish
fruit
(orange) juice
meat
milk
onions
pasta
(baked) potato
rice
(spinach) salad
(tuna) sandwich
soda
(vegetable) soup
spaghetti
steak
tea
tomato (sauce)
vegetable

breakfast
lunch
dinner

hungry
meal

Speaking Strategy

Talking about likes and dislikes
Do you like (Indian) food?
Do you like (fish)?

Yes! I love it!
Yes, I like it a lot.
Yeah, it's OK.
No, not really.
No, I can't stand it.

LESSON B

Vocabulary

bananas
cancer
(a) cold
energy
good for you ↔ bad for you
have / eat breakfast
healthy ↔ unhealthy
**high (in) ↔ low (in) (calories /
  sugar / protein)**
honey
ice
ice cream
illness
junk food
medicine
milk
oranges
skin
skip (breakfast)
snack
stomach
strawberries
taste good ↔ taste bad
vitamins
yogurt

UNIT 6 RELATIONSHIPS

LESSON A

Vocabulary

grandparents
grandmother
grandfather

parents
mother
father

(older) sister
(younger) brother

aunt
uncle
cousin

wife
husband
daughter
son
baby
children

Speaking Strategy

**Asking and answering
  questions about family**
How many people are (there) in
your family?
  (There are) four: me, my brother,
  and my parents.

Do you have any brothers and
sisters?
  Yes, I have a sister. / No, I'm an
  only child.

Are you close (to your sister)?
  Yes, I am. / No, not really.

LESSON B

Vocabulary

boyfriend
(be) dating / seeing someone
girlfriend
ex-husband / wife
(be) married
(be) single

Talking about relationships
marriage (n)
marry, get married (v)
(be) married (adj)

divorce (n)
divorce, get divorced (v)
(be) divorced (adj)

Talking about age
How old are you?
  I'm... (years old).

10 ten	24 twenty-four
11 eleven	25 twenty-five
12 twelve	26 twenty-six
13 thirteen	27 twenty-seven
14 fourteen	28 twenty-eight
15 fifteen	29 twenty-nine
16 sixteen	30 thirty
17 seventeen	40 forty
18 eighteen	50 fifty
19 nineteen	60 sixty
20 twenty	70 seventy
21 twenty-one	80 eighty
22 twenty-two	90 ninety
23 twenty-three	100 one hundred

UNIT 7 TIME

LESSON A

Vocabulary

wake up
take a shower
get dressed
leave home
start (class)
finish (class)
study
go home
do homework
go to bed

two (o'clock)
two-oh-five / five after two
two fifteen / quarter after two
two thirty / half past two
two forty-five / quarter to three
two fifty-five / five to three

in the morning / afternoon / evening
at noon / midnight
at night

yesterday / today / tonight / tomorrow

early / late

Speaking Strategy

Making suggestions
Let's see a movie.
We could see a movie.

Saying yes
(That) sounds good.
Good / Great idea.

Saying no politely
I don't really like French food.
I don't really want to see that movie.

LESSON B

Vocabulary

(a) day off
go dancing, shopping
go for a walk, bike ride, run
go out with friends, family, your boyfriend or girlfriend
go to the movies, gym, beach, a club, concert, party, friend's house
(on) the weekend
spend time with (someone)

UNIT 8 SPECIAL OCCASIONS

LESSON A

Vocabulary

January
February
March
April
May
June
July
August
September
October
November
December

ordinal numbers: first, second, third, fourth, etc.

When were you born?
I was born...
spring, summer, fall / autumn, winter

Speaking Strategy

Saying you know or don't know something
Is tomorrow a holiday?
Yes, it is. / No, it isn't.
I'm not sure. It could be.
I don't (really) know.
When is Labor Day?
It's on September 3rd this year.
I'm not sure. Is it in September?
I don't (really) know.

LESSON B

Vocabulary

annual
attend
celebrate
compete
event
festival (art, film, food, holiday, music, sport, spring, summer, autumn, winter)
miss
parade
perform
take photos
take place
traditional

Saying how often something happens
daily, weekly, monthly, annually
every two / three / four years

UNIT 9 COME TOGETHER

LESSON A

Vocabulary

clean your room
do chores / the housework
do / wash the dishes
do the grocery shopping
do the laundry
**empty the trash / take out the
 garbage**
make a snack
make breakfast / lunch / dinner
make the bed

Speaking Strategy

Apologizing
Making an apology
(I'm) sorry.
(I'm) sorry about that.
I'm really sorry.

Responding to an apology
Don't worry (about it).
That's OK / all right.
No problem.
Apology accepted.

LESSON B

Vocabulary

break up (with someone)
couple
hang out (with someone)
invite
meet

Expressions with *date*
verb + *date*: **ask on** a date, **be
 on** a date, **go on** a date, **have**
 a date
adjective + *date*: **blind** date,
 first date

UNIT 10 HOME

LESSON A

Vocabulary

air conditioner (A/C)
balcony
bathroom
bed
bedroom
chair
closet
dining room
elevator
garage
kitchen
lamp
living room
oven
refrigerator
rent
rug
shower
sink
sofa
stairs
table
toilet
wall
window
yard

Speaking Strategy

Showing surprise
My house has 20 rooms.
 Really? / Are you serious? / For
 real?
Yeah.

My house has 20 rooms.
 You're kidding. / You're joking. /
 No way.
(No,) it's true.

LESSON B

Vocabulary

Colors
black
(dark / light) blue
brown
gray
green
orange
pink
purple
red
white
(bright) yellow

Feelings
relaxed ↔ nervous,
 uncomfortable
happy ↔ unhappy, sad

save energy / water / money
turn on ↔ turn off the TV, the
 lights, the A/C

UNIT 11 CLOTHING

LESSON A

Vocabulary

CLOTHING
blouse
coat
dress
jacket
jeans
pants
pullover
shirt
shorts
skirt
socks
suit
sweater
T-shirt
uniform

SHOES
boots
heels
sandals
sneakers

ACCESSORIES
belt
gloves
hat
scarf

a pair of (earrings)

jewelry
rings
window-shopping

Speaking Strategy

Saying what you want
I'm looking for a gift for my sister.

Asking for and giving prices
How much are they?
   They're 60 euros.
Thanks, I'll think about it.
How much is the T-shirt?
   It's 19 euros.
I'll take it.

When you're not looking for
   anything in particular:
Can I help you?
   No thanks, I'm just looking.

LESSON B

Vocabulary

baggy / loose ↔ fitted / tight
casual ↔ dressy / formal
heavy ↔ light
long ↔ short
put on ↔ take off
style

change clothes
cover fit
match
protect
suitable
tie
try on (clothes, shoes, glasses)

UNIT 12 JOBS

LESSON A

Vocabulary
businessperson
cashier
chef
delivery person
doctor
flight attendant
hairstylist
lawyer
nurse
police officer
programmer
receptionist
reporter
telemarketer
tutor
waiter / waitress
web designer

business card

Speaking Strategy

Talking about jobs
What do you do?
What does he / she do?

I'm a student / programmer / doctor.
He's a waiter. / She's a nurse.
I work for Telefonica / Bank of China / DHL Global Mail / myself.
She works in a hospital / an office / a cafe.

LESSON B

Vocabulary
do an internship
(have, get) experience
(have a) full-time ↔ part-time job
(work) full time ↔ part time
get a job
goal
make money
pay

Using large numbers / Talking about pay

I want to make… (dollars) a (year).

1,000	one thousand
2,000	two thousand
10,000	ten thousand
50,000	fifty thousand
100,000	one hundred thousand
150,000	one hundred fifty thousand
500,000	five hundred thousand / half a million
1,000,000	one million
1,000,000,000	one billion

UNIT **1** INTRODUCTIONS

LESSON A

Subject Pronouns with *be*			
Subject pronoun	***be***		**Subject pronoun contractions with *be***
I	**am**		I am = I'm
You	**are**	a student.	you are = you're
He / She	**is**		he is = he's / she is = she's
We / They	**are**	students.	we are = we're / they are = they're
It	**is**	a book.	it is = it's

Possessive Adjectives with *be*			
Possessive adjective		***be***	
My			
Your	last name	**is**	Smith.
His / Her			
Our / Their			
Its	title	**is**	*World Link.*

A Complete each sentence with the correct form of the verb *be*.

1. She _____ a teacher.
2. It _____ an ID card.
3. You _____ my classmate.
4. I _____ here.

B Look at the underlined words. Then write the correct subject pronoun.

1. <u>Yuki and Beto</u> are here.
   _____ are here.
2. <u>My ID card</u> is at home.
   _____ is at home.
3. <u>Lily</u> is at school.
   _____ is at school.
4. <u>Carlos</u> is at home.
   _____ is at home.

C Complete the sentences with the correct subject pronoun or possessive adjective.

1. _____ is a teacher. _____ name is Mr. Porter.
2. _____ are my cousins. _____ last name is Novak.
3. _____ name is Yukiko. _____ nickname is Yuki.
4. _____ is a teacher. _____ name is Ms. Groves.

D Rewrite each sentence on a separate piece of paper. Use a contraction.

1. I am a student.
2. You are my classmate.
3. She is a teacher.
4. It is an ID card.
5. They are my classmates.
6. He is a student.

LESSON B

Yes / No Questions with *be*			Short Answers	
be	Subject pronoun		Affirmative	Negative
Am	I	in this class?	Yes, you are.	No, you**'re not**.* / No, you **aren't**.
Are	you	a student?	Yes, I am.	No, **I'm not**.
Is	he / she		Yes, he is.	No, he**'s not**.* / No, he **isn't**.
Is	it	her real name?	Yes, it is.	No, it**'s not**.* / No, it **isn't**.
Are	we	in this class?	Yes, we are.	No, we**'re not**.* / No, we **aren't**.
Are	they	students?	Yes, they are.	No, they**'re not**.* / No, they **aren't**.

*In spoken English, this negative form is more common.

A Read each question. Circle the correct answer.

1. Is your name John?   a. No, it's not.   b. No, I'm not.

2. Are you from Canada?   a. No, you're not.   b. No, I'm not.

3. Is Ms. Kim the teacher?   a. Yes, she is.   b. Yes, it is.

4. Are you friends with Jane?   a. Yes, I am.   b. Yes, I'm friends.

5. Am I late for class?   a. No, it's not.   b. No, you aren't.

6. Are Yuki and Carlos your friends?   a. Yes, we are. b. No, they're not.

Dae Sung ("Danny") Park

His good friends Vanessa and Milo

B Look at the photos. Complete the questions and answers. Then ask and answer them with a partner.

1. __Is__ his nickname Dae Sung?   ___No___, it's ___Danny___.

2. _____ baseball _____ sport?   No, _____. _____ is his favorite.

3. _____ Vanessa and Milo his friends?   _____.

4. _____ Vanessa his girlfriend?   _____, they're just friends.

5. _____ you friends with Danny?   No, _____.

UNIT 2 COUNTRIES

LESSON A

Questions with *who*			Answers	
Who	is 's	he / she ?	He's / She's my classmate.	*Who* asks about people.
		from Mexico? with you?	Tomas (is).	
	are	you? they?	(I'm) Sara. (They're) my friends.	

Questions with *where*			Answers	
Where	are	you / they?	(I'm / We're / They're) **at** school / work / home. **at** the beach / a museum.	*Where* asks about a place. Use *at* + a place. Use *in* / *from* + a city or country.
Where	is 's	Nor?	(She's) **in** London / **at** her hotel.	
		Machu Picchu?	(It's) **in** Peru.	
		Ryan from?	(He's) **from** Australia.	

A Complete the questions and answers with *who, where, in,* or *at* and information from the chart.

Name	Hometown	Where is he or she now?
Emma ♀	Berlin, Germany	on vacation / Mexico
Hisham ♂	Rabat, Morocco	on vacation / Italy
Jun ♂	Beijing, China	Mei's house
Mei ♀	Beijing, China	home
Tim ♂	Toronto, Canada	work / New York City

1. __Who__ is from Rabat?   Hisham is.

2. _____'s Rabat?   It's ____ Morocco.

3. Where is Hisham now?   He's _____.

4. _____ is Emma from?   She's _____.

5. Who's ____ the US now?   _____.

6. _____ exactly is Tim?   He's ____ work ____ New York City.

7. Where are Mei and Jun?   They _____.

8. Who's on vacation now?   _____.

B 🗣 Write three new *who* or *where* questions about the information in the chart. Ask a partner the questions.

	be	Adjective	Adjectives with *be*
Your city	**is**	beautiful.	Adjectives are words that describe nouns.
The buildings	**are**	old.	Adjectives follow *be*.
Carnival	**is**	fun and loud.	Use *and* to join two adjectives.

	be		Adjective	Noun	
It	**is**	an	exciting	city.	Adjectives can come before nouns.
There	**are**	many	tall	buildings.	Use *a* or *an* before singular nouns.

A Circle the adjectives and underline the nouns.

1. It's a crowded place.

2. Are you a busy person?

3. They are tall and beautiful.

4. She's a friendly teacher.

5. Our street is busy and interesting.

6. My small town is famous for good food.

B Put the words in parentheses into the sentences. Write the new sentences.

1. He's English teacher. (an)

   _____.

2. The restaurant is small friendly. (and)

   _____.

3. That student is in class. (new)

   _____.

4. It's a city of five million people. (large)

   _____.

5. There's a view from the mountain. (wonderful)

   _____.

6. It's a big city with the feeling of a town. (small)

   _____.

UNIT 3 POSSESSIONS

LESSON A

Singular and Plural Count Nouns				
It's	**an**	ID card.		Count nouns have singular (= one thing) and plural (= two or more things) forms.
I'm	**a**	student.		
There are ten		students	here.	Use *a* or *an* before singular count nouns only.

When the singular noun begins with a consonant sound, use *a*.
When the singular noun begins with a vowel sound, use *an*.

Spelling Rules for Forming Plural Nouns		
Most plural nouns are formed by adding *s*:	camera → camera**s**	pen → pen**s**
For nouns ending in a <u>vowel</u> + *y* add *s*:	b**oy** → boy**s**	
but For nouns ending in a <u>consonant</u> + *y*, drop the *y* and add *ies*:	diction**ary** → dictionar**ies**	
For nouns ending in a <u>vowel</u> + *o* add *s*:	rad**io** → radio**s**	
but For nouns ending in a <u>consonant</u> + *o*, add *s* with some nouns and *es* with others:	pho**to** → photo**s**	pota**to** → potato**es**
For nouns ending in the *ch, sh, ss,* or *x* sounds, add *es*:	cla**ss** → class**es**	
For nouns ending in *f* or *fe*, change it to *ve* + *s*:	kni**fe** → kni**ves**	lea**f** → lea**ves**

A In your notebook, complete the sentences with the words below. With a partner, practice saying them aloud without looking at your book. Remember to use *a* or *an* for singular words.

1. It's _____.
2. They're _____.

backpack	city	gift card	notebook	teacher
knife	credit card	student ID	pen	umbrella
potato	dictionary	key	photo	wallet
cell phone	email address	laptop	student	watch

B Complete the sentences with the singular or plural form of the noun in parentheses. Then ask and answer the questions with a partner.

1. What's in your backpack?

   There's (cell phone) _____, (laptop) _____, and (bus pass) _____.

2. What's in your wallet?

   There's (student ID) _____, two (photo) _____, and two (credit card) _____.

3. What's on your desk?

   There are three (pen) _____, (notebook) _____, and two (dictionary) _____.

this / that / these / those		
A: What's **this** called in English? B: It's (called) a "cell phone."	A: Bill, **this** is my friend Nadia. B: Hi, Nadia. Nice to meet you.	Use **this** to talk about a thing or person near you.
A: Is **that** a new phone? B: Yes, it is.	A: Who's **that** (over there)? B: That's my friend Leo.	Use **that** to talk about a thing or person away from you.
A: Are **these** your keys? B: No, they're not.	A: Yuki, **these** are my parents. B: Nice to meet you.	Use **these** to talk about two or more things or people near you.
A: **Those** headphones are cool. B: Yeah, they are.	A: What are **those**? B: They're my new earrings.	Use **those** to talk about two or more things or people away from you.

A Look at the photos. Complete the questions and answers.

1. A: Is _____ your new tablet?
   B: Yes, _it is_.
   A: It's nice.

2. A: Excuse me! Are _____ your keys?
   B: Yes, _____.
      Thanks.

3. A: Who's _____?
   B: My teacher. Let's go and say hello.

4. A: Are _____ your sunglasses over there?
   B: No, _____. My sunglasses are in my backpack.

5. A: Eva, _____ is Bill.
   B: Hi, Bill. Nice to meet you.

B 🔁 Practice the dialogs in **A** with a partner.

LESSON A

The Present Continuous Tense: Affirmative and Negative Statements				
Subject pronoun	*be*	*(not)*	**verb + -ing**	**Contractions with *be***
I	**am**			I am = I'm; I am not = I'm not
You	**are**	*(not)*	**working.**	you are = you're; you are not = you're not / you aren't
He / She / It	**is**			she is = she's; she is not = she's not / she isn't
We / They	**are**			we are = we're; we are not = we're not / we aren't

The Present Continuous Tense: *Wh-* Questions and Answers and *Yes / No* Questions and Answers				
Question word	*be*	**subject**	**verb + -ing**	**Answers**
What	are	you	**doing**?	(I'm) **exercising**.
	is	he		(He's) **exercising**.
	are	they		(They're) **exercising**.
Where	are	you	**sitting**?	(We're) **sitting** in the front.
	be	**subject**	**verb + -ing**	**Short answers**
	Are	you		Yes, I am. No, I'm not. I'm **texting**.
	Is	she	**studying**?	Yes, she is. No, she's not. / No, she isn't. She's **reading**.
	Are	you		Yes, we are. No, we're not. / No, we aren't. We're **swimming**.
		they		Yes, they are. No, they aren't. / No, they're not. They're **working**.

Spelling rules for verb + *ing*

In most cases, add *ing* to the base form of the verb: *work → working*

If the verb ends in an *e*, drop the *e* and add *ing*: *exercise → exercising*

If the verb has one syllable and ends in a consonant + vowel + consonant, double the final consonant and add *ing*: *sit → sitting* (This does not apply if the verb ends in *w, x,* or *y*: *row → rowing*.)

A Complete the sentences with the appropriate words. Use contractions where possible.

1. A: ___*Are*___ you (take) ___*taking*___ the bus?

   B: No, _____. I (walk) _____.

2. A: What _____ they (do) _____ at the gym?

   B: They _____ (run) _____ and (swim) _____.

3. A: _____ you (use) _____ this computer?

   B: No, we _____. We (talk) _____.

4. A: Where _____ she (study) _____?

   B: At the English lab. She (listen) _____ to questions and (write) _____ the answers.

5. A: _____ he still (sleep) _____?

   B: No, he _____. He _____ already (work) _____.

LESSON B

The Present Continuous Tense: Extended Time	
A: What **are** you **doing** <u>right now</u>? B: I**'m studying** for a test <u>at the moment</u>.	You can use the present continuous to talk about actions happening now, at the moment of speaking. Notice the <u>time expressions</u>.
A: What **are** you **doing** <u>these days / nowadays</u>? B: I**'m studying** in Hong Kong <u>this term</u>. A: **Are** you **enjoying** Hong Kong? B: Yes, I**'m having** a great time!	You can also use the present continuous to talk about actions continuing for a period of time in the present. Notice the <u>time expressions</u>.

A Monika is traveling in Ecuador for a month. Read her email to a friend. Complete the sentences with the present continuous tense.

Hi Kira,

(1. I / write) _____ to you from Ecuador. Today, (2. our group / visit) _____ Quito, the capital city. It's really beautiful. Right now, (3. we / eat) _____ lunch. The food here is so good!

(4. I / enjoy) _____ this program. This week, (5. we / learn) _____ about the rainforest and the animals in Ecuador. (6. I / also / use) _____ my Spanish a lot, and that's great. There's only one bad thing: (7. it / rain) _____ a lot these days. But (8. the rain / not / stop) _____ us. We are outside every day.

Well, (9. we / leave) _____ the cafe now, so that's all my news for today. (10. you / do) _____ anything fun this month?

Write soon,

Monika

B Answer the questions. Write the numbers (1–10) from **A** on the correct line.

Which sentences in **A** are about…

1. actions happening right now? _____

2. actions continuing for a period of time in the present? _____

UNIT **5** **FOOD**

LESSON A

The Simple Present Tense: Affirmative Statements	
Subject pronoun	**Verb**
I / You / We / They	eat
He / She / It	eats

(meat.)

The Simple Present Tense: Negative Statements					Contractions with *do*
Subject pronoun	***do***	*not*	**Verb**		
I / You / We / They	**do**	(not)	eat	meat.	do not = don't
He / She / It	**does**				does not = doesn't

Spelling rules for third person singular (*he, she, it*)

In most cases, add *s* to the base form of the verb: *eat → eats*

If the base form ends in *s, sh, ch, x, or z*, add *es*: *tea<u>ch</u> → teaches*

If the base form ends in consonant + *y*, change the *y* to *i* and add *es*: *stu<u>dy</u> → studies*

If the base form ends in consonant + *o*, add *es*: *g<u>o</u> → goes   d<u>o</u> → does*

The verb *have* is irregular: *have → has*

A Complete the sentences. Use the simple present tense.

1. Maria (live) _____ in Barcelona, but her parents (live) _____ in a small town. Of course, she (speak) _____ Spanish. She also (understand) _____ some French, but she (not / speak) _____ it well.

2. Duncan (teach) _____ at a cooking school. Sarah (go) _____ to school there, and she (enjoy) _____ it. School (finish) _____ at 3:00. After school, Sarah (hurry) _____ from campus to her part-time job. She (work) _____ in a restaurant.

3. In my family, we (not / use) _____ a fork and knife. We (use) _____ chopsticks to eat our meals. We (have) _____ rice every day. My little brother (have) _____ milk every morning. My mother (not / drink) _____ milk. She (drink) _____ coffee every morning.

B 🔁 Rewrite the information in **A** (item 3) above so that it is true for you and your family. Then share it with a partner.

Simple Present *Yes / No* Questions				
do	Subject	Verb	Short answers	Contractions with *do*
Do	you		Yes, I do. / No, I don't.	do not = don't
Does	he / she	like spicy food?	Yes, he / she does. / No, he / she doesn't.	does not = doesn't
Do	you		Yes, we do. / No, we don't.	do not = don't
	they		Yes, they do. / No, they don't.	

A Complete the questions and answers.

1. ___Do___ you like spicy food?   No, _____.

2. _____ they speak English?   Yes, _____.

3. _____ he have breakfast every day?   No, _____.

4. _____ we have a test today?   Yes, _____.

5. _____ your mother cook well?   Yes, _____.

6. _____ you and your boyfriend eat lunch together? No, _____.

B 🔁 Complete the dialogs with *Yes / No* questions and answers. Then practice with a partner.

1. A: What are you eating?

   B: Pasta with chocolate sauce.

   A: Really? (it / taste) _____ good?

   B: Yes, _____. (you / want) _____ some?

2. A: (you / know) _____ Jamie Oliver?

   B: No, _____. Who is he?

   A: He's a famous chef from England.

   B: Oh yeah! (he / have) _____ a show on TV?

   A: _____. It's on Channel 4.

3. A: My parents want to go to a nice restaurant. (you / know) _____ a good place?

   B: (they / like) _____ spicy food?

   A: Yeah, my dad _____, but my mom _____.

   B: Oh, okay. Well, (they / eat) _____ sushi?

   A: _____. They love it.

   B: Try Umami Sushi. It's a good place.

C 🔁 Write short answers to the questions on a piece of paper. Then compare your answers with a partner's.

1. Do you want to try the pasta with chocolate sauce?

2. Do you know Jamie Oliver or other famous chefs?

3. Do your parents like spicy food? How about sushi? Do you?

LESSON A

Possessive Nouns		
Singular nouns (+ 's)	**Plural nouns (+ ')**	**Irregular plural nouns (+ 's)**
sister → sister**'s** brother → brother**'s**	parents → parent**s'** brothers → brother**s'**	children → children**'s** women → women**'s**
For first and last names that end in *s*, you can add **'s** or just **'**.		

A Look up the word *twin* in a dictionary. Read about Hallie Parker and Annie James from the movie *The Parent Trap.* Complete the sentences with a singular noun, a plural noun, or a possessive noun.

1. Hallie Parker lives in her (father) _____ home in California, in the US.

2. Annie (James) _____ home is in London. She lives there with her (mother) _____.

3. The two (girl) _____, Hallie and Annie, are (twin) _____! But they live apart.
   They don't know about each other.

4. (Hallie) _____ summer plans are exciting. She's going to summer camp. And by chance,
   (Annie) _____ is going to the same summer camp!

5. At camp, Hallie sees her (sister) _____ face for the first time. They look the same! They are
   both surprised and happy.

6. Hallie doesn't know her (mom) _____ name, and Annie doesn't know her (dad)
   _____ name.

7. Before the two (child) _____ leave camp, they have an idea. The two (sister) _____ plan
   is an exciting one!

B What do you think happens next? Write three sentences. Tell your partner.

_____.

_____.

_____.

LESSON B

Have got			
I've / You've / We've / They've	got	a big family. a nice apartment. a lot of free time. black hair.	I've got = I have got He's got = He has got
He's / She's			

Have got means the same as *have,* but is used in certain situations. You can use *have got* or *have* to talk about relationships, things you own or have, your schedule, or how something looks. It's usually used with the *have* or *has* contracted.

But only use *have* (not *have got*) in these kinds of cases:

I **have** breakfast.   (NOT: ~~I've got breakfast...~~)

I **have** fun with my friends.   (NOT: ~~I have got fun...~~)

A Complete the sentences with *have got* or *has got*.

1. Paolo isn't single. He _____ a girlfriend.

2. I _____ an older sister and a younger brother.

3. Mom isn't home now. She _____ a doctor's appointment today.

4. My sister and I can't go to the party. We _____ a lot of homework.

5. Akemi's parents live in Japan. They _____ a beautiful house there.

6. You _____ six classes this term? Wow, you're busy!

B Read the sentences. Can you use both *have* and *have got*? Or can you only use *have*? Circle the correct answer(s).

1. A: I have / 've got a question. Is Linda an only child?

   B: No, she has / 's got a brother and sister.

2. A: Do you want something to drink?

   B: Can I have / 've got a glass of water, please?

3. A: Is there a party at Nina's house?

   B: Yes, she has / 's got a party every year for her birthday.

4. A: Is your sister's degree in English?

   B: No, she has / 's got a degree in business.

UNIT **7** TIME

LESSON A

Prepositions of Time		

When is your class?	It's **on** Monday.
	    on Mondays. (every Monday)
	    on Tuesday night.
		day of the week

	It's **in** the morning / afternoon / evening. It's **at** night.	period of the day
	It's **at** 8:30. **at** noon.	specific time
	It's **from** 4:00 **to** 5:30. **from** Tuesday **to** Saturday.	length of time (start to finish)

A Read about Lucia's schedule. Fill in the blanks with *in, on, at, from,* or *to.*

1. My name is Lucia. I'm a nurse. I work _____ Monday _____ Friday.

2. I work in the hospital _____ night. My shift is _____ midnight _____ 9:30 _____ the morning.

3. On workdays, I go to bed _____ 3 PM and wake up _____ 10 PM.

4. I do my grocery shopping _____ the afternoon and _____ Saturdays.

5. It's difficult because my husband works _____ 9 AM _____ 6 PM every day. I don't see him a lot.

6. _____ Sundays, we are both off. We like to go to the park together and relax.

B What do you think of Lucia's schedule? Tell a partner.

C Think of another night job. Answer the questions about the job. Look online to learn more. Then tell a partner.

1. Which days do you work in this job? _____

2. What time does the job start and finish? _____

3. Is the job easy or difficult? _____

LESSON B

Simple Present *Wh-* Questions				
Question word	*do / does*	Subject	Verb	Answers
Who	do	you	study with?	(I study with) Maria.
What	does	she	do on Saturdays?	(She) goes out with friends.
When	do	they	have class?	(They have class) at 8:00.
		we		(We have class) on Mondays.
Where	does	he		(He has class) in Room 3B.

A Read each item. Then use the words in parentheses and information in the responses to complete the questions.

1. A: Who (you) _____*do you live*_____ with?
   B: I live with my sister.

2. A: When (your brother) _____ in the morning?
   B: He wakes up at 7:15.

3. A: Where (your grandparents) _____?
   B: They live in London.

4. A: What time (this class) _____?
   B: It ends at 2:30.

5. A: When (we) _____ a test in this class?
   B: We have a test tomorrow.

6. A: What (you) _____ on the weekends?
   B: I go out with my friends.

B ✂ Ask a partner the questions in **A**.

UNIT **8** SPECIAL OCCASIONS

LESSON A

Prepositions of Time: *in* and *on*		
When is the holiday party?	It's **on** December 20th. It's **on** Christmas Eve. It's **on** Monday.	Use *on* before days of the week, dates, and holidays.
	It's **in** the morning / afternoon / evening. It's **in** December. It's **in** the winter. It's **in** (early / late) 2016.	Use *in* before times of day, months, seasons, and years.

A Complete these sentences with the correct prepositions.

1. In my city, schools are closed _____ Christmas Day. This year, Christmas is _____ Thursday so we have Friday off, too!

   In my family, we get up _____ the morning and open presents. We have a big holiday meal _____ the afternoon. It's a fun day!

2. The Olympics are _____ the summer and _____ the winter. _____ 2020, the Summer Olympics are in Tokyo. They begin _____ July 24th. _____ 2018, the Winter Olympics are in South Korea. They begin _____ February.

3. Many countries have Father's Day _____ the third Sunday _____ June. _____ Father's Day in Venezuela, families come together and have lunch.

LESSON B

	When and How long Questions	
With be	**When** is the festival?	It's **in** July / **on** Thursday. It starts **on** July 1 / **at** 10:00.
	How long is the festival?	(It's) **from** July 1 **to** July 3. (It lasts) **until** July 3. **for** three days.
With other verbs	**When** do you study?	(I study) **on** Saturdays / **in** the evening.
	How long do you study?	(I study) **from** 4:00 to 6:00. **until** 6:00. **for** an hour.

A *When* question usually asks for specific time information—a specific day, month, or time of day. But sometimes, it can ask about a length of time. For example, it's possible to ask "When is the festival?" and answer "It's from July 1 to 3."
How long only asks about a length of time.

A 🔄 Circle the correct words in the dialogs. There may be more than one correct answer. Then practice them with a partner.

1. A: When / How long do you work today?

   B: From / For / To 4:00 for / to / at 8:00.

2. A: When / How long is our holiday break?

   B: It starts in / on / at the ninth.

3. A: When / How long are you staying in London?

   B: Until / For / To January third.

4. A: When / How long does vacation last?

   B: From / Until / For a month.

B 🔄 Complete each dialog with a *When* or *How long* question, or an answer.

Event	Dates
Summer break	June 19–September 19
The school festival	April 1–7
Department store holiday hours	Every day, 8:00 AM–midnight

1. A: When does summer break start?

   B: _____

2. A: _____

   B: Summer break lasts for three months.

3. A: _____

   B: It ends on April 7.

4. A: _____

   B: The festival lasts _____.

5. A: _____
   B: The department store opens _____.

6. A: How late is the store open?
   B: _____

7. A: How long is the store open every day?
   B: _____

LESSON A

Frequency Adverbs		

with *be*	Jackie <u>is</u> **always** late for class. 100%
	     usually
	     often
	     sometimes
	     hardly ever
	     never 0%
		Frequency adverbs come after the verb *be.*

with other verbs	Sandra **always** <u>makes</u> dinner.	With other verbs, most frequency adverbs come before the main verb.
sometimes* and *usually	Stuart **sometimes** empties the trash. **Sometimes** Stuart empties the trash. Stuart empties the trash **sometimes**.	***Sometimes*** and ***usually*** can also come at the beginning or the end of a sentence.
with *not*	Marco isn't **usually** late for class. Marco doesn't **usually** make his bed. Marco **sometimes** doesn't make his bed.	Frequency adverbs come after *not.* Except for **sometimes**. Don't put **sometimes** after *not.*

A Minerva is a maid. Unscramble the words to read about her job.

1. 10 AM / usually / 4 PM / I / from / visit / to

   _____.

2. busy / I / am / sometimes / very

   _____.

3. work / I / always / on holidays / don't

   _____.

4. I / dishes / wash / never

   _____.

5. a vacation / take / hardly ever / I

_____ .

6. often / a tip / people / give me

_____ .

B ✏ Make the statements true for you. Write a frequency adverb in the first space. Then complete each sentence. Share your answers with a partner.

1. In the morning, I _____ forget my _____ .

2. On the weekend, I _____ go to _____ .

3. I _____ make a snack of _____ after school.

4. I _____ do the laundry at home.

5. I _____ study _____ hours before a big exam.

LESSON B

Review: Simple Present *Wh-* Questions				
Question word	***do / does***	**Subject**	**Verb**	**Answers**
Who	do	you	like?	(I / We like) Maria.
What			do on the weekend?	(I / We) hang out with friends.
Where			go on dates?	(I / We go to) the movies.
Why			go there?	It's fun.
When	does	class	start?	(It starts at) 9:30.
How long			last?	(It lasts for) two hours.

You can also use *who* to ask these kinds of questions:

Who has a boyfriend?   *Erin does. / I do.*

A Read the unfinished questions and the answers. Then complete each *Wh-* question.

1. A: Who _____?

   B: Yang likes Jenny.

2. A: When _____ in your country?

   B: People go on a first date at age 18 or 19.

3. A: Where _____ on a first date?

   B: Most college students go to a movie.

4. A: How long _____?

   B: Usually a first date lasts three or four hours.

5. A: What _____ on the weekend?

   B: I hang out with my friends.

6. A: Why _____?

   B: Some couples break up because they are unhappy.

B   🗨 Ask a partner questions 2–6 in **A**. Give your own answers.

UNIT 10   HOME

LESSON A

<table>
<tr><th colspan="4">There is / There are</th></tr>
<tr><th>There is / isn't</th><th></th><th colspan="2">Singular noun</th></tr>
<tr><td>There is (There's)</td><td>a / an
one</td><td>chair / air conditioner
closet</td><td rowspan="2">in my bedroom.</td></tr>
<tr><td>There is
There isn't</td><td>no
a / an</td><td>balcony
garage / elevator</td></tr>
<tr><th>There are / aren't</th><th></th><th colspan="2">Plural noun</th></tr>
<tr><td>There are</td><td>— / four / some / many</td><td rowspan="2">elevators</td><td></td></tr>
<tr><td>There are
There aren't</td><td>no
any</td><td>in that building.</td></tr>
</table>

Use *there is / there are* to say that something does or doesn't exist, or to say its location.
there's is the contracted form of *there is. There are* does not have a contracted form.

Questions	Short answers
Is there an elevator in your building?	Yes, **there is**. / No, **there isn't**.
Are there (any) windows in your living room?	Yes, **there are**. / No, **there aren't** (any).
How many windows **are** (**there**) in your bedroom?	**There's** one. / **There are** two. / **There aren't** any.

A   Read about the Winchester Mystery House. Complete the sentences with *there's, there isn't, there are,* or *there aren't.*

(1.) _____ a big, strange house in California: the Winchester Mystery

House. (2.) _____ about 160 rooms in the house, including 40 bedrooms,

and (3.) _____ three elevators. (4.) _____ stairs and doors that go

nowhere. (5.) _____ a special room in the house. (6.) _____ only

one door that goes into the room, but (7.) _____ three doors that exit it.

(8.) _____ a beautiful garden and a large bell. Many tourists visit the house.

(9.) _____ tours during the day, but (10.) _____ any tours at night.

(11.) _____ an easy way to get out—so be careful! Don't get lost!

B 🔊 Complete the questions about the Winchester Mystery House. Then ask and answer them with a partner.

1. _____ rooms are there in the house?

2. _____ any elevators?

3. _____ bedrooms are there?

4. _____ a garden?

5. _____ bells are there?

6. _____ tours at night?

LESSON B

			very / too			
	Verb	*a / an*	*very / too*	**Adjective / Adverb**	**Noun**	*to* + **Verb**
❶ This room	is		**very / too**	dark.		
❷ He	talks		**too**	fast. I don't understand.		
❸ I	am		**too**	tired		to watch TV.
❹ They	have	a	**very**	big	house.	

❶ *Very* and *too* make adjectives and adverbs stronger.

❷ Use *too* when something is more than you need or want and there is <u>a negative result</u>.
   ☞*He talks **too** fast. <u>I can't understand him</u>. / This room is **too** dark, and <u>I can't see</u>.*

❸ Use *too* with this pattern (*too* + verb).
   ☞*I'm **too tired to watch** TV. I'm going to bed.*

❹ Use *very* to modify an adjective + noun: *They have **a very big house**.*
   Don't use *too*: ~~They have a too big house.~~

A Complete the sentences with *very* or *too.*

1. It's _____ noisy in here. I can't hear you. Let's go outside.

2. This is a _____ beautiful color. Let's use it in the dining room.

3. These chairs are _____ old, but we can still use them.

4. This dorm room is _____ small for four people. Four students can't live in here.

5. My neighbor is a _____ nice person. I like him a lot.

6. We're _____ late for the movie. It started at 7:00, and now it's 8:20. It's almost over.

7. He lives in a _____ large apartment; it's almost 400 square meters!

8. I'm _____ tired to walk to the fifth floor. I'm taking the elevator.

9. The rent here is $1,000 a month. That's _____ expensive for me. I can only pay $800.

10. These apartments are _____ expensive, but a lot of people buy them.

B Complete the sentences with *very* or *too* and your ideas. Then explain your answers to a partner.

1. My bedroom is _____.

2. I'm too old to _____.

3. I'm too young to _____.

4. English is _____.

5. Right now, it's _____ early to _____.

UNIT 11 CLOTHING

LESSON A

want to / have to					
Subject	*want / want to*	**Base form**	**Noun**	**Second sentence**	
I	**want**		these boots.	They're cool.	These sentences have almost the same meaning. Only the form is different.
	want to	buy			
Subject	*have / have to*	**Base form**	**Noun**	**Second sentence**	
I	**have**		a coat.	It's in the closet.	Use *have* + noun to show possession.
	have to	buy		I don't have one.	Use *have to* to say something is necessary.

A Complete the sentences with *to*. If *to* isn't needed, don't write anything.

1. I have _____ a test tomorrow. I have _____ study tonight.
2. Does Aya want _____ a new jacket for her birthday?
3. Diego doesn't have _____ wear a suit on Fridays. He can wear jeans.
4. Cleo wants _____ buy a new dress for the party.
5. I don't have _____ money for the bus. Do you?
6. Martin has _____ class at 9:00 AM. He has _____ leave home by 8:00.
7. Do you want _____ see a movie tonight?
8. My parents want _____ visit China this summer. Do they have _____ get a visa?

B 🔁 Make the sentences true for you. Complete each one with *(don't) want to* or *(don't) have to*. Share your answers with a partner.

1. I _____ study English.
2. I _____ wear jeans on the weekend.
3. I _____ stay at school every day until 3 PM.
4. I _____ wear a uniform to school.
5. I _____ buy some new clothes.

LESSON B

Count Nouns	Noncount Nouns	
This **shirt is** / These **shirts are** expensive.	This **clothing is** expensive.	Count nouns can be singular or plural. Noncount nouns are always singular.
This ring is **a dollar / two dollars**.	I want to save **money**. (Not: ~~a money~~)	Only count nouns can have *a*, *an*, or a number in front of them.
I need (**some**) new winter **boots**.	I need (**some**) **luggage** for my trip.	Both count and noncount nouns can use *some*.
I have **a pair of sunglasses**. He has **ten pairs of shoes** in his closet.	**a piece of / two pieces of jewelry** **a cup of / two cups of coffee** **a glass of / two glasses of water**	You can use *a pair of* to count items that are always plural (*pants, glasses, pajamas, headphones*) and items that come in twos (*shoes, gloves, earrings*). You can also make some noncount nouns countable by adding words like *a piece of, a cup of, a glass of*.

Some common noncount nouns:
- Collective items: *clothing, jewelry, money, luggage, furniture*
- Certain food and drink items: *bread, rice, fruit, meat, water, coffee, tea, milk*
- Abstract ideas: *life, time, love, information, evidence*

A 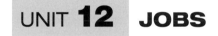 Complete the dialogs with *a(n)* or nothing. Then practice with a partner.

1. A: Your dad wears _____ jewelry, right?

   B: Yes. He wears _____ wedding ring.

2. A: I need _____ new pair of gloves. Let's go shopping.

   B: I can't. I have _____ homework.

3. A: Can I have _____ money for the bus?

   B: Sure. Here's _____ dollar.

4. A: I need _____ information about fashion design classes.

   B: There's _____ link on the school website. Check it out.

5. A: I'm bringing _____ luggage on the plane. Are you?

   B: Yeah, I have _____ small bag.

B 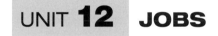 Imagine you are going to Lima for a week. Make a list of clothes and other items you need. Finish the sentences with count or noncount nouns. Then compare your ideas with a partner.

1. I need some _____ for my trip.

2. I also have to get _____ and some _____.

3. And finally, I need a(n) _____, two _____, and a pair of _____.

> I have to get some snacks for the plane.

UNIT **12** JOBS

LESSON A

Questions with *like*	
A: My mom works in a hospital. B: Really? **What's** that **like**? A: It's hard, but she enjoys it.	You can use *like* to ask questions about an experience. In this question, *that = working in a hospital.*
A: My coworker is from Brazil. B: Oh? **What's** he **like**? A: He's really nice / friendly / outgoing / smart.	You can also use *like* to ask questions about a person and his or her personality. *What's (he) like?* *What are (they) like?*

A Complete the dialogs with the correct questions.

1. A: Ms. Collins is my math teacher this term.

   B: Oh? _____

   A: She's really nice.

2. A: I'm a student at Stanford University.

   B: Really? _____

   A: It's a great school. I love it.

3. A: My brother works in an office.

   B: _____

   A: Sometimes it's boring, but he likes it.

4. A: My tutor is from London.

   B: Really? _____

   A: He's very friendly.

LESSON B

Talking about Ability with *can / can't*		
I / You / He / She / We / They	**can / can't**	speak French.

Can and *can't* are followed by the base form of the verb.

Can't is the short form of *cannot*. In spoken English, *can't* is more common.

Questions with *can / can't*		
Yes / No questions	**Can** you speak Spanish?	Yes, I **can**. / No, I **can't**.
Wh- questions	Which languages **can** Carla speak?	(She **can** speak) Spanish and English.
	Who **can** speak Japanese?	Toshi (**can**).

A Complete the dialogs with a question or answer with *can* or *can't*.

1. A: Can Mario drive?

   B: No, _____. He's only 14.

2. A: _____?

   B: Yes, I can. I'm a good driver.

3. A: _____?

   B: No, Jun's parents can't speak English.

4. A: _____?

   B: Yes, Linda can swim, but her sister _____.

B Make questions and answers about Adam and Sonya using *can* and the words given.

> **Adam:** musician
>
> **Languages:** English and Chinese
>
> **Hobbies:** I like to ski and play guitar.
>
> **Sonya:** programmer
>
> **Languages:** Spanish and English
>
> **Hobbies:** I like to dance and ski.

1. Who / speak Chinese? _____

   Adam can speak Chinese. _____

2. What / languages / Sonya / speak? _____

   _____

3. Who / build / websites? _____

   _____

4. What / instrument / Adam / play? _____

   _____

5. Who / ski? _____

   _____

C 🎧 Ask and answer the questions in **A** and **B** aloud with a partner.

Answers

Communication page 23

1. Brasilia **2.** Chinese **3.** FREE **4.** United Arab Emirates **5.** Cairo **6.** New York City **7.** FREE **8.** Russia **9.** Chile **10.** Answers will vary. **11.** FREE **12.** Jakarta **13.** The British Royal Family **14.** Germany **15.** Thai **16.** FREE **17.** Kuala Lumpur, Malaysia **18.** Venice **19.** English, French **20.** Austria **21.** Brazil, Colombia, Peru, Bolivia, Venezuela, Ecuador **22.** FREE **23.** Answers will vary.

Speaking page 113, C

1. c **2.** b **3.** c **4.** a